Activities Manual/Study Guide

to accompany

Looking Out/Looking In

N I N T H   E D I T I O N

Ronald Adler
Neil Towne

Prepared by

Mary O. Wiemann

Santa Barbara City College

Harcourt Brace College Publishers

Fort Worth   Philadelphia   San Diego   New York   Orlando   Austin   San Antonio
Toronto   Montreal   London   Sydney   Tokyo

CONTENTS

Chapter 6 *Nonverbal Communication: Messages Without Words* 141

Chapter 7 *Listening: More than Meets the Ear* 163

PREFACE

Welcome to the *Activities Manual/Study Guide* for *Looking Out/Looking In,* Ninth Edition. Responding to feedback from *Activities Manual* users around the country, this *Activities Manual/Study Guide* is designed to enhance student learning. The *Activities Manual/Study Guide* contains more than 50 class-tested exercises and more than 500 study test items designed to build understanding of principles and proficiency in skills introduced in the text.

Each chapter in the *Activities Manual/Study Guide* parallels the chapter in *Looking Out/Looking In.* The following areas in each chapter combine to provide a thorough, student-centered learning package:

• **Outlines** Extended outlines of each chapter begin each section. Many instructors ask students to use the outlines as a lecture guide in class or a place to take notes as they read the chapter.

• **Key Terms** Vocabulary terms for each chapter follow the outlines; they are spaced so that students can write in definitions for each term in the *Study Guide.* This helps students study for exams and focus on important concepts.

• **Activities** Students who complete the activities in this manual will develop understanding and skill in each area through a choice of exercises. Exercises are coded with icons to help you choose how to use them. ❖ denotes a group activity. ◆ identifies an individual one.

> *Skill Builder* activities–designed primarily to help students identify the target behavior in a number of common interpersonal communication situations. These are frequently group activities that reinforce learning in the classroom. They can be done as individual activities.

> *Invitation to Insight* activities–designed to help students discover how newly learned principles can be applied in their everyday lives. They can be grouped together to form a "Communication Journal" for the entire course. While these activities are usually designed for individual use, they can provide the structure for small group discussion or lecture/discussion.

> *Oral Skill* activities–designed to allow students to actually exhibit communication behaviors they have studied. They are designed for individual, dyadic, or small group use in a classroom or lab setting.

Many of the activities can be used in a variety of ways. Instructors can adapt them, use some or all, grade them or leave them ungraded, assign them as out-of-class exercises, or use them as class enrichment. Student observations in many exercises will lead to class discussions on how to apply the newly learned principles in the "real world" of one's interpersonal relationships.

While they almost always stimulate class discussion, the activities in this manual are designed to do more than keep a class busy or interested. If they are used regularly, they will help students to move beyond simply understanding the principles of interpersonal communication and actually to perform more effectively in a variety of communication situations.

Study Guide activities–designed to help students identify major concepts or skills contained in the chapter. They are designed to be done individually, in groups, or with the entire class, and they have answer keys found at the end of each chapter. Vocabulary Crossword Puzzles, True/False, Completion, and Multiple Choice items review and reinforce for students as they work at their own pace.

I would like to thank the following people for the insights and comments they provided on the creation of this edition of the *Activities Manual/Study Guide:* Carol Davis, Oakton Community College; Todd Harrison, Iowa Western Community College; Diana Hutchinson, Scottsdale Community College; and Jo Ann Lawlor, West Valley College.

The *Activities Manual/Study Guide* should help develop more effective communication, both in class and in students' lives outside the classroom. Students who go through the outlines, fill in the key terms, and complete the study guides do better on quizzes and tests than those who fail to complete some or all of these aids. The greatest satisfaction, however, comes from using the activities in this manual to develop more effective communication with loved ones, co-workers and friends.

Mary Wiemann

Chapter 1

A First Look at Interpersonal Relationships

OUTLINE

Use this outline to take notes as you read the chapter in the text and/or as your instructor lectures in class.

I. Introduction to interpersonal communication

A. Communication Is Important

B. Why We Communicate
 1. Physical needs
 2. Identity needs
 3. Rubin's social needs
    a. Pleasure
    b. Affection
    c. Inclusion
    d. Escape
    e. Relaxation
    f. Control
 4. Practical goals
    a. Instrumental goals
    b. Maslow's basic needs
       1) Physical
       2) Safety
       3) Social
       4) Self-esteem
       5) Self-actualization

II. The process of communication

A. A Linear View
 1. Sender
 2. Encoding
 3. Message
 4. Channel
 5. Decoding
 6. Receiver

7. Noise
   a. External (physical)
   b. Physiological
   c. Psychological
8. Environments

B. A Transactional View
1. Feedback is verbal and nonverbal
2. We send/receive messages simultaneously
3. Nonisolated "acts" are involved
4. Behaviors are verbal and nonverbal

III. Communication principles and misconceptions

A. Communication Principles
1. Communication is *with* others, not *to* them
2. Communication can be intentional or unintentional
3. Communication is irreversible
4. Communication is unrepeatable

B. Avoiding Communication Misconceptions
1. Meanings are not in words
2. More communication is not always better
3. No single person or event causes another's reaction.
4. Communication will not solve all problems
5. Communication is not a natural ability

IV. The nature of interpersonal communication

A. Two Views of Interpersonal Communication
1. Quantitative–dyadic
2. Qualitative
   a. Uniqueness
   b. Irreplaceability
   c. Interdependence
   d. Disclosure
   e. Intrinsic rewards
   f. Scarcity

B. Personal and Impersonal Communication: A Matter of Balance

V. Communicating about relationships

A. Content and Relational Messages

B. Metacommunication

C. Types of Relational Messages
1. Affinity
2. Respect
3. Control
   a. Types
      (1) Decisional
      (2) Conversational

2 CHAPTER ONE   A FIRST LOOK AT INTERPERSONAL RELATIONSHIPS

Harcourt Brace & Company

      b. Distribution
          (1) Complementary
          (2) Symmetrical
          (3) Parallel

VI. Communication competence: What makes an effective communicator?

A. Communication Competence Defined
1. No "ideal" way to communicate
2. Competence is situational
3. Competence is relational

B. Characteristics of Competent Communicators
1. A wide range of behaviors
2. The ability to choose the most appropriate behavior
   a. Context
   b. Your goal
   c. Your knowledge of the other person
3. Skill at performing behaviors
   a. Beginning awareness
   b. Awkwardness
   c. Skillfulness
   d. Integration
4. Cognitive complexity
5. Self-monitoring
6. Commitment to the relationship
   a. Commitment to the other person
   b. Commitment to the message

KEY TERMS

Use these key terms to review major concepts from your text. Write the definition for each key term in the space to the right.

affinity _____

awareness _____

awkwardness _____

behavior _____

channel _____

cognitive complexity _____

commitment _____

Harcourt Brace & Company

communication_____

communication competence _____

communication misconceptions_____

communication model _____

communication principles_____

complementary relationship _____

content message _____

context_____

control_____

conversational control_____

decision control _____

decoding_____

dyad _____

dyadic communication _____

encoding_____

environment _____

escape _____

external noise _____

feedback _____

impersonal communication _____

inclusion_____

influence_____

instrumental goals _____

integration _____

Harcourt Brace & Company

interpersonal communication (quantitative and qualitative) _____

interpersonal relationship _____

intimacy _____

linear communication model _____

message _____

metacommunication _____

needs (physical, identity, social) _____

noise (external, physiological, psychological) _____

parallel relationship _____

physiological noise _____

pleasure _____

practical goals _____

psychological noise _____

receiver _____

relational message _____

relaxation _____

respect_____

self-actualization _____

self-monitoring _____

sender _____

skillfulness_____

symmetrical relationship _____

transactional communication model_____

Harcourt Brace & Company

ACTIVITIES

1.1 COMMUNICATION SKILLS INVENTORY

◆ Activity Type: Invitation to Insight

PURPOSES

1. To help you discover how satisfied you are with the way you communicate in various situations.
2. To preview some topics that will be covered in *Looking Out/Looking In.*

INSTRUCTIONS

1. Below you will find several communication-related situations. As you read each item, imagine yourself in that situation.
2. For each instance, answer the following question: *How satisfied am I with the way I would behave in this situation and ones like it?* You can express your answers by placing one of the following numbers in the space by each item:

5 = Completely satisfied with my probable action
4 = Generally, though not totally, satisfied with my probable action
3 = About equally satisfied and dissatisfied with my probable action
2 = Generally, though not totally, dissatisfied with my probable action
1 = Totally dissatisfied with my probable action

_____ 1. A new acquaintance has just shared some personal experiences with you that make you think you'd like to develop a closer relationship. You have experienced the same things and are now deciding whether to reveal these personal experiences. (8)

_____ 2. You've become involved in a political discussion with someone whose views are the complete opposite of yours. The other person asks, "Can't you at least understand why I feel as I do?" (3, 7)

_____ 3. You are considered a responsible adult by virtually everyone except one relative who still wants to help you make all your decisions. You value your relationship with this person, but you need to be seen as more independent. You know you should do something about this situation. (9, 10)

_____ 4. In a mood of self-improvement a friend asks you to describe the one or two ways by which you think he or she could behave better. You're willing to do so, but need to express yourself in a clear and helpful way. (3, 5, 10)

_____ 5. A close companion says that you've been behaving "differently" lately and asks if you know what he or she means. (5, 6, 7)

_____ **6.** You've grown to appreciate a new friend a great deal lately, and you realize that you ought to share your feelings. (4)

_____ **7.** An amateur writer you know has just shown you his or her latest batch of poems and asked your opinion of them. You don't think they are very good. It's time for your reply. (5, 9, 10)

_____ **8.** You've found certain behaviors of an important person in your life have become more and more bothersome to you. It's getting harder to keep your feelings to yourself. (4, 10)

_____ **9.** You're invited to a party at which everyone except the host will be a stranger to you. Upon hearing about this, a friend says, "Gee, if I were going I'd feel like an outsider. They probably won't have much to do with you." How do you feel? (2)

_____ **10.** A friend comes to you feeling very upset about a recent incident and asks for advice. You suspect that there is more to the problem than just this one incident. You really want to help the friend. (7)

_____ **11.** You find yourself defending the behavior of a friend against the criticisms of a third person. The critic accuses you of seeing only what you want to see and ignoring the rest. (2, 4, 5, 9, 10)

_____ **12.** A boss or instructor asks you to explain a recent assignment to a companion who has been absent. You are cautioned to explain the work clearly so there will be no misunderstandings. (5)

_____ **13.** You ask an acquaintance for help with a problem. She says yes, but the way the message is expressed leaves you thinking she'd rather not. You do need the help, but only if it's sincerely offered. (6, 10)

_____ **14.** A roommate always seems to be too busy to do the dishes when it's his or her turn, and you've wound up doing them most of the time. You resent the unequal sharing of responsibility and want to do something about it. (10)

_____ **15.** A new acquaintance has become quite interested in getting to know you better, but you feel no interest yourself. You've heard that this person is extremely sensitive and insecure. (1, 2)

You can use the results of this survey in two ways. By looking at each question you can see how satisfied you are with your behavior in that specific type of situation. A response of 1 or 2 on any single question is an obvious signal that you can profit from working on that situation. Parenthetical numbers following each item indicate the chapters of _Looking Out/Looking In_ which focus on that subject.

By totaling your score for all of the items you can get an idea of how satisfied you are with your overall ability to communicate in interpersonal situations. A score of 68–75 suggests high satisfaction, 58–67 indicates moderate satisfaction, while 45–57 shows that you feel dissatisfied with your communication behavior nearly half the time.

Another valuable way to use this activity is to make a second inventory at the end of the course. Have you improved? Are there still areas you will need to work on?

1.2 EXPANDING YOUR COMMUNICATION EFFECTIVENESS

◆ Activity Type: Invitation to Insight

PURPOSES

1. To help you broaden your repertoire of effective communication behaviors and your skill at performing them.
2. To help you identify the most appropriate communication behaviors in important situations.

INSTRUCTIONS

1. Use the space below to identify two areas in which you would like to communicate more effectively.
2. For each area, identify a person you have observed who communicates in a way that you think would improve your effectiveness. Describe this person's communication behavior.
3. Describe how you could adapt these behaviors to your own life.

Example

a. Area in which you would like to communicate more effectively: *Making conversation with people I've just met.*
b. Model who communicates effectively in this area: *My friend Rich*
c. Model's behavior: *He asks sincere questions of people he's just met, compliments them enthusiastically, and smiles a lot.*
d. How could you apply these behaviors? *I can spend more time thinking about people I've just met and less time thinking self-consciously about my own nervousness. Then I can focus on parts of these new people that interest me and let the other person know I'm interested. The key seems to be sincerity: I have to really mean what I say and not use questions and compliments as tricks.*

SITUATION 1

a. Area in which you would like to communicate more effectively

_____

b. Model who communicates effectively in this area _____

c. Model's behavior_____

_____

d. How could you apply these behaviors? _____

_____

_____

SITUATION 2

a. Area in which you would like to communicate more effectively

_____

b. Model who communicates effectively in this area _____

c. Model's behavior_____

_____

d. How could you apply these behaviors? _____

_____

_____

_____

SITUATION 3

a. Area in which you would like to communicate more effectively

_____

b. Model who communicates effectively in this area _____

c. Model's behavior_____

_____

d. How could you apply these behaviors? _____

_____

_____

_____

Harcourt Brace & Company

1.3 RECOGNIZING RELATIONAL MESSAGES

◆❖ Activity Type: Skill Builder

PURPOSES

1. To illustrate that virtually every message has both a content and a relational dimension.
2. To give you practice recognizing the relational dimension of common messages.
3. To demonstrate that relational messages are ambiguous and need to be verified by perception-checking statements.

INSTRUCTIONS

1. Describe the relational issues that seem to be involved in each of the situations listed below.
2. Record examples of your own messages and identify the relational levels involved.

CONTENT LEVEL	RELATIONAL LEVEL (INCLUSION, CONTROL, AFFECTION, RESPECT)
Example: *Students and instructor disagree about whether testing and grading system is fair.*	**Control:** *Students' right to help shape courses.* **Respect:** *Whether instructor values opinions of students.*
1. A friend asks if you want to come over and share a bottle of wine.	
2. Wife complains that husband doesn't help out enough around the house.	
3. Boss asks if your hours are working out.	
4. Couple argues about whose family to visit over holidays.	
5. Friend A teases friend B in good-natured way about B's bad memory.	
6. Employees object to management's requirement that all illnesses be verified by a doctor's note.	

Harcourt Brace & Company

CONTENT LEVEL	RELATIONAL LEVEL (INCLUSION, CONTROL, AFFECTION, RESPECT)
7. Parent to child: "You'll make the right decision."	
8. Romantic partner says, "When you're late, I feel angry and disappointed and I worry if something's happened."	
9. Parents remind teenager to drive carefully every time he or she goes out.	
10. Doctor's receptionist puts you on hold for five minutes when you call to make an appointment.	
11. Teen says to parent, "You can't make me do anything."	
12. Mother asks, "You're going to wear that?"	
13. A friend hangs up on you after arguing on the phone.	
14. Boss rolls eyes and sighs when you ask if you can take time off.	
15. Girlfriend asks boyfriend how he feels about their relationship.	
Now, record examples of messages you've sent or that were sent to you (content)–and identify the relational dimension(s) of the message.	
16.	
17.	
18.	

Harcourt Brace & Company

CROSSWORD PUZZLE

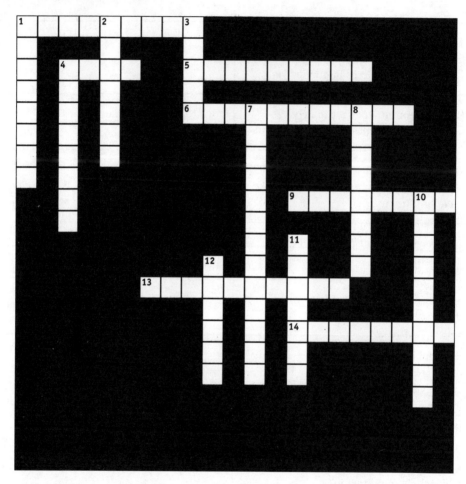

Across

1 the social need to care for others and to be cared for by them
4 two individuals communicating
5 the social need to feel a sense of belonging in some relationship with others
6 the field of experiences that leads a person to make sense of another's behavior
9 the discernible response of a receiver to sender's message
13 behavior that treats others as objects rather than as individuals
14 one who notices and attends to a message

Down

1 the degree to which persons like to appreciate one another
2 the medium through which a message passes from sender to receiver
3 any force that interferes with effective communication
4 the process during which a receiver attaches meaning to a message
7 communication in which the parties consider one another as unique individuals rather than as objects
8 the process of putting thoughts into symbols, most commonly words
10 the communication ability to accomplish one's personal goals in a manner that maintains a relationship on terms that are acceptable to all parties
11 the social need to influence others
12 the creator of a message

TRUE/FALSE

Mark the statements below as true or false. Correct statements that are false on the lines below to create a true statement.

_____ 1. Studies show your physical health may be affected by communication.

_____

_____ 2. People with high self-esteem are confident in themselves, so they are more likely to seek out people who treat them poorly as a test of their confidence.

_____

_____ 3. Communication skills are more important in helping you get a job than in keeping the job or performing it well.

_____

_____ 4. Instrumental goals are the same thing as social needs.

_____

_____ 5. Psychologist Abraham Maslow claims that basic needs must be satisfied before people concern themselves with higher order needs.

_____

_____ 6. The linear view of communication suggests that communication flows in one direction, from sender to receiver.

_____

_____ 7. The transactional model of communication shows that communication is something we do *to* others.

_____

_____ 8. No single person or event causes another's reaction.

_____

_____ 9. Luckily, communication will always help us solve our problems.

_____

_____ **10.** Dyadic communication is the earliest form of interaction we experience and the most common type of communication.

_____

_____ **11.** What qualifies as competent behavior in one culture might be completely inept, or even offensive, in another.

_____

_____ **12.** In order to build a competent relationship, we need to get rid of our need to maintain some space between ourselves and the other person.

_____

_____ **13.** You can build competent relationships only if you put the other person's needs ahead of yours.

_____

_____ **14.** Effective communicators are able to choose their actions from a wide range of behaviors.

_____

_____ **15.** Just knowing about communication skills makes you a better communicator.

_____

COMPLETION

Fill in the blanks below with the correct terms chosen from the list below.

instrumental goals   social needs   identity needs   physiological noise
psychological noise   self-monitoring   control   commitment
cognitive complexity   empathy

1. _____ are the needs we have to define who we are.

2. _____ are the needs we have to link ourselves with others.

3. _____ are the needs we have to get others to behave in ways we want.

4. _____ refers to the forces within a communicator that interfere with the ability to express or understand a message accurately.

5. _____ refers to the biological factors in the receiver or sender that interfere with accurate reception of messages.

6. _____ is the degree to which the parties in a relationship have the power to influence one another.

7. _____ is the desire to interact and continue the relationship.

8. _____ is the ability to view issues in the relationship in a variety of different ways.

9. _____ is the process of paying close attention to your behavior in order to shape the way you behave.

10. _____ is the ability to take the other person's perspective in a relationship.

MULTIPLE CHOICE

Choose the letter of the communication process element that is most illustrated by the description found below. Italicized words provide clues.

  a. encode
  b. decode
  c. channel
  d. message/feedback
  e. noise (external, physiological or psychological)
  f. environment

_____ **1.** The children make a *videotape* of themselves to send to their grandparents instead of writing a *letter*.

_____ **2.** Marjorie tries to decide the best way to tell Martin that she can't go to Hawaii with him.

_____ **3.** Martin decides Marjorie means she doesn't love him when she says she can't go to Hawaii.

_____ **4.** It's so hot in the room that Brad has a hard time concentrating on what his partner is telling him.

_____ **5.** Linda *smiles* while Larry is talking to her.

_____ **6.** Brooke is daydreaming about her date while Allison is talking to her.

_____ **7.** Since Jacob has never been married, it's difficult for him to understand why his married friend Brent wants to spend less time with him.

_____ **8.** Whitney says, *"I'm positive about my vote."*

_____ **9.** Richard *thinks* Jon wants to leave when he waves to him.

_____ **10.** Laura *winks* when she *says* she's serious and *gestures* with her arms.

_____ **11.** Erin is from a wealthy family and Kate from a poor one. They have a serious conflict about how to budget their money.

_____ **12.** Jack has been feeling a cold coming on all day while he has sat through the meeting.

_____ **13.** Levi constructs the best arguments to convince his parents to buy him a new car.

_____ **14.** Jessica decides to lie to her group members about the reason she missed the meeting last night.

_____ **15.** "I refuse to go," said Jeremy.

Choose the *best* answer for each of the questions below:

16. According to a contextual definition of interpersonal communication, interpersonal communication occurs when

    a. two people interact with one another, usually face to face.
    b. you watch a TV show about relationships.
    c. you read a romance novel.
    d. your romantic partner leaves a message on your answering machine.

17. All of the following statements are true <u>except</u>

    a. Communication can be intentional.
    b. Communication is irreversible.
    c. Communication can be unintentional.
    d. Communication is repeatable.

18. All of the following statements are true <u>except</u>

    a. Meanings are not in words.
    b. More communication is not always better.
    c. Communication can solve all your problems.
    d. Communication is not a natural ability.

19. The messages people exchange about their relationship are termed

    a. affinity.
    b. metacommunication.
    c. complementary symmetry.
    d. communication competence.

20. When you are able to perform communication skills without thinking about them, you have entered the skill stage of

    a. awareness.
    b. awkwardness.
    c. skillfulness.
    d. integration.

CROSSWORD PUZZLE

Across and down filled grid:

- 1 across: affection
- 1 down: affinity
- 2 down: channel
- 3 down: nose (noss)
- 4 across: dyad
- 4 down: decoding
- 5 across: inclusion
- 6 across: environment
- 7 down: interpersonal
- 8 down: encoding
- 9 across: feedback
- 10 down: competence
- 11 down: control
- 12 down: sender
- 13 across: impersonal
- 14 across: receiver

TRUE/FALSE

1. T	**4.** F	**7.** F	**10.** T	**13.** F
2. F	**5.** T	**8.** T	**11.** T	**14.** T
3. F	**6.** T	**9.** F	**12.** F	**15.** F

Harcourt Brace & Company

COMPLETION

1. identity needs
2. social needs
3. instrumental goals
4. psychological noise
5. physiological noise
6. control
7. commitment
8. cognitive complexity
9. self-monitoring
10. empathy

MULTIPLE CHOICE

1. c
2. a
3. b
4. e
5. d
6. e
7. f
8. d
9. b
10. c
11. f
12. e
13. a
14. a
15. d
16. a
17. d
18. c
19. b
20. d

Harcourt Brace & Company

Chapter 2

Communication and the Self

OUTLINE

Use this outline to take notes as you read the chapter in the text and/or as your instructor lectures in class.

I. Communication and the self-concept

A. **Definition: The Relatively Stable Set of Perceptions You Hold of Yourself**

B. **How the Self-Concept Develops**
   1. Reflected appraisal (through significant others)
   2. Social comparison (through reference groups)

C. **Characteristics of the Self-Concept**
   1. The self-concept is subjective
      a. Obsolete information
      b. Distorted feedback
      c. Emphasis on perfection
      d. Social expectations
   2. The self-concept resists change
      a. Change-not-acknowledged problem
      b. Self-delusion/lack of growth problem

D. **Culture and the Self-Concept**
   1. Language
   2. Individualistic versus collective identities

E. **The Self-Fulfilling Prophecy and Communication**
   1. Definition: expectations held that make an outcome more likely
   2. Types
      a. Self-imposed
      b. Imposed by others
   3. Influence
      a. Improve relationships
      b. Damage relationships

F. **Changing Your Self-Concept**
   1. Have realistic expectations
   2. Have realistic perceptions

3. Have the will to change
4. Have the skill to change

II. Presenting the self: Communication as identity management

A. Public and Private Selves
1. Perceived self
2. Presenting self
   a. facework
   b. self-monitoring

B. Characteristics of Identity Management
1. We strive to construct multiple identities
2. Identity management is collaborative.
3. Identity management can be deliberate or unconscious.

C. Why Manage Identities?
1. Social rules
2. Personal goals
3. Relational goals

D. How Do We Manage Identities?
1. Manner
   a. Words
   b. Nonverbal behavior
2. Appearance
3. Setting
   a. Face to face
   b. Mediated

E. Identity Management and Honesty

KEY TERMS

Use these key terms to review major concepts from your text. Write the definition for each key term in the space to the right.

appearance_____

cognitive conservatism _____

collective identity _____

distorted feedback _____

ego booster_____

ego buster_____

face_____

front_____

identity management _____

individualistic identity _____

manner _____

myth of perfection _____

obsolete information _____

perceived self_____

presenting self_____

reference groups_____

reflected appraisal _____

self-concept _____

self-fulfilling prophecy _____

self-monitor_____

self-verification_____

setting _____

significant other _____

social comparison _____

social expectations_____

Harcourt Brace & Company

ACTIVITIES

2.1 WHO DO YOU THINK YOU ARE?

◆ Activity Type: Invitation to Insight

PURPOSE

To help you identify your own self-concept.

INSTRUCTIONS

1. For each category below, supply the words or phrases that describe you best.
2. After filling in the spaces within each category, organize your responses so that the most fundamental characteristic is listed first, with the rest of the items following in order of descending importance.

PART A: IDENTIFY THE ELEMENTS OF YOUR SELF-CONCEPT

1. What moods or feelings best characterize you (cheerful, considerate, optimistic, etc.)?

   a. _____   b. _____   c. _____

2. How would you describe your physical condition and/or your appearance (tall, attractive, weak, muscular, etc.)?

   a. _____   b. _____   c. _____

3. How would you describe your social traits (friendly, shy, aloof, talkative, etc.)?

   a. _____   b. _____   c. _____

4. What talents do you possess or lack (good artist, lousy carpenter, competent swimmer, etc.)?

   a. _____   b. _____   c. _____

5. How would you describe your intellectual capacity (curious, poor reader, good mathematician, etc.)?

   a. _____   b. _____   c. _____

6. What beliefs do you hold strongly (vegetarian, Christian, passivist, etc.)?

   a. _____   b. _____   c. _____

Harcourt Brace & Company

7. What social roles are the most important in your life (brother, student, friend, bank teller, club president, etc.)?

   a. _____   b. _____   c. _____

8. What other terms haven't you listed so far that describe other important things about yourself?

   a. _____   b. _____   c. _____

PART B: ARRANGE YOUR SELF-CONCEPT ELEMENTS IN ORDER OF IMPORTANCE

1. _____   13. _____

2. _____   14. _____

3. _____   15. _____

4. _____   16. _____

5. _____   17. _____

6. _____   18. _____

7. _____   19. _____

8. _____   20. _____

9. _____   21. _____

10. _____   22. _____

11. _____   23. _____

12. _____   24. _____

NOTE: You will use these descriptors in 2.3.

Harcourt Brace & Company

2.2 EGO BOOSTERS AND BUSTERS

◆ Activity Type: Invitation to Insight

PURPOSES

1. To help you identify how significant others have shaped your self-concept.
2. To help you realize how you shape the self-concept of others.

INSTRUCTIONS

1. In the appropriate spaces below describe the actions of several "ego boosters": significant others who shaped your self-concept in a positive way. Also describe the behavior of "ego busters" who contributed to a more negative self-concept.
2. Next, recall several incidents in which you behaved as an ego booster or buster to others. Not all ego boosters and busters are obvious. Include in your description several incidents in which the messages were subtle or nonverbal.
3. Summarize the lessons you have learned from this experience by answering the questions at the end of this exercise.

EGO BOOSTER MESSAGES YOU HAVE RECEIVED

Example

I perceive(d) _my chem. lab partner_ as telling me I am/was ___attractive___ when he or
           (significant other)   (self-concept element)

she *keeps (kept) sneaking glances at me and smiling during our experiments.* _____

1. I perceive(d) _____ as telling me I am/was
                                (significant other)
_____ when he/she _____
    (self-concept element)

_____

_____

_____

2. I perceive(d) _____ as telling me I am/was
                                (significant other)
_____ when he/she _____
    (self-concept element)

_____

_____

_____

3. I perceive(d) _____ as telling me I am/was
                                       (significant other)

_____ when he/she _____
        (self-concept element)

_____

_____

EGO BUSTER MESSAGES YOU HAVE RECEIVED

Example

I perceive(d) _my neighbor_ as telling me I am/was _not an important friend_ when
                   (significant other)   (self-concept element)

he/she _had a big party last weekend and didn't invite me._ _____ _____

1. I perceive(d) _____ as telling me I am/was
                                       (significant other)

_____ when he/she _____
        (self-concept element)

_____

_____

2. I perceive(d) _____ as telling me I am/was
                                       (significant other)

_____ when he/she _____
        (self-concept element)

_____

_____

3. I perceive(d) _____ as telling me I am/was
                                       (significant other)

_____ when he/she _____
        (self-concept element)

_____

_____

Harcourt Brace & Company

EGO BOOSTER MESSAGES YOU HAVE SENT

Example

I was a booster to _my instructor_ when I _told her I enjoyed last Tuesday's lecture._

1. I was a booster to _____ when I _____

_____

_____

2. I was a booster to _____ when I _____

_____

_____

3. I was a booster to _____ when I _____

_____

_____

EGO BUSTER MESSAGES YOU HAVE SENT

Example

I was a buster to _my sister_ when I _forgot to phone her or send even a card on her_

birthday.

1. I was a buster to _____ when I _____

_____

2. I was a buster to _____ when I _____

_____

_____

3. I was a buster to _____ when I _____

_____

_____

Harcourt Brace & Company

CONCLUSIONS (USE AN ADDITIONAL SHEET OF PAPER IF NECESSARY)

Who are the people who have most influenced your self-concept in the past? What messages did each one send to influence you so strongly?

_____

_____

_____

_____

What people are the greatest influences on your self-concept now? Is each person a positive or a negative influence? What messages does each one send to influence your self-concept?

_____

_____

_____

_____

Who are the people whom *you* have influenced most greatly? What messages have you sent to each one about his or her self-concept? How have you sent these messages?

_____

_____

_____

_____

What ego booster or buster messages do you want to send to the important people in your life? How can you send each one?

_____

_____

_____

_____

2.3 SELF-CONCEPT INVENTORY

◆ Activity Type: Invitation to Insight

PURPOSE

1. To give you a clearer picture of how you see yourself (your perceived self).
2. To illustrate how others perceive you (presenting self).

INSTRUCTIONS

1. Transfer the list of 24 elements of your self-concept from 2.1 to index cards (or strips of paper). If you didn't do 2.1, go back and complete that now.
2. Arrange your cards in a stack, with the one that *best* describes you at the top and the one that *least* describes you at the bottom.
3. Using the Perceived Self column (Table 1), record the order in which you arranged the cards (1 is the most like you). You will leave out some cards or add on to your list on the opposite page.
4. Cover your Perceived Self column and ask two other people (a friend, co-worker, roommate, family member, classmate) to arrange the descriptors in an order in which they see you. Record these perceptions in Tables 2 and 3, being sure to cover your own Table 1 and the Table 2 or 3 that the other person has worked on (so no one sees what the other has written). Record the name/relationship of your evaluator at the top of the appropriate column.
5. Compare the three tables, circling any descriptors that differ from column to column.
6. Answer the questions at the end of this exercise.

TABLE 1 PERCEIVED SELF	TABLE 2 PRESENTING SELF TO	TABLE 3 PRESENTING SELF TO
	(RELATIONSHIP TO YOU)	(RELATIONSHIP TO YOU)
1. _____	1. _____	1. _____
2. _____	2. _____	2. _____
3. _____	3. _____	3. _____
4. _____	4. _____	4. _____
5. _____	5. _____	5. _____

Harcourt Brace & Company

6. _____	6. _____	6. _____
7. _____	7. _____	7. _____
8. _____	8. _____	8. _____
9. _____	9. _____	9. _____
10. _____	10. _____	10. _____
11. _____	11. _____	11. _____
12. _____	12. _____	12. _____
13. _____	13. _____	13. _____
14. _____	14. _____	14. _____
15. _____	15. _____	15. _____
16. _____	16. _____	16. _____
17. _____	17. _____	17. _____
18. _____	18. _____	18. _____
19. _____	19. _____	19. _____
20. _____	20. _____	20. _____
21. _____	21. _____	21. _____
22. _____	22. _____	22. _____
23. _____	23. _____	23. _____
24. _____	24. _____	24. _____

Describe any factors that have contributed in a positive or negative way to the formation of your perceived self (obsolete information, social expectations, perfectionistic beliefs). Include any other factors involved in the formation of your perceived self (for example, certain significant others, any strong reference groups).

_____

_____

_____

_____

Harcourt Brace & Company

Describe any differences between your perceived self and the ways your evaluators perceived you (your presenting selves). What factors contribute to the differences in perception? Whose view is the most accurate and why?

_____

_____

_____

_____

_____

Why might your partners in this exercise view you differently from the way you perceive yourself? Would other people in your life view you like either of the people in this exercise? Give some specific examples with reasons why they would or would not have a similar perception.

_____

_____

_____

_____

_____

Harcourt Brace & Company

2.4 REEVALUATING YOUR "CAN'TS"

◆ Activity Type: Invitation to Insight

PURPOSE

To help you identify and eliminate any self-fulfilling prophecies which hamper effective communication.

INSTRUCTIONS

1. Complete the following lists by describing communication-related difficulties you have in the following areas.
2. After filling in each blank space, follow the starred instructions that follow the list (*).

DIFFICULTIES YOU HAVE COMMUNICATING WITH FAMILY MEMBERS

Examples

I can't *discuss politics with my dad without having an argument*
because *he's so set in his ways.*

I can't *tell my brother how much I love him*
because *I'll feel foolish.*

1. I can't_____

   because _____

2. I can't_____

   because _____

* Corrections (see instructions at end of exercise)

_____

_____

DIFFICULTIES YOU HAVE COMMUNICATING WITH PEOPLE AT SCHOOL OR AT WORK

Examples

I can't *say "no" when my boss asks me to work overtime*
because *he'll fire me.*

Harcourt Brace & Company

I can't *participate in class discussions even when I know the answers or have a question* because *I just freeze up.*

1. I can't_____

   because _____

2. I can't_____

   because _____

* Corrections (see instructions at end of exercise)

_____

_____

DIFFICULTIES YOU HAVE COMMUNICATING WITH STRANGERS

Examples

I can't *start a conversation with someone I've never met before* because *I'll look stupid.*

I can't *ask smokers to move or stop smoking* because *they'll get mad.*

1. I can't_____

   because _____

2. I can't_____

   because _____

* Corrections (see instructions at end of exercise)

_____

_____

DIFFICULTIES YOU HAVE COMMUNICATING WITH FRIENDS

Examples

I can't *find the courage to ask my friend to repay the money he owes me* because *I'm afraid he'll question our friendship.*

I can't *say no when friends ask me to do favors and I'm busy* because *I'm afraid they'll think I'm not their friend.*

Harcourt Brace & Company

1. I can't_____

　　because _____

2. I can't_____

　　because _____

* Corrections (see instructions at end of exercise)

_____

_____

DIFFICULTIES YOU HAVE COMMUNICATING WITH YOUR ROMANTIC PARTNER (PAST OR PRESENT)

Examples

I can't *tell Bill to wear a tie to the party*
because *he'll laugh at me.*

I can't *bring up going to visit my parents*
because *we'll fight.*

1. I can't_____

　　because _____

2. I can't_____

　　because _____

* Corrections (see instructions at end of exercise)

_____

_____

*After you have completed the list, continue as follows:

a. Read the list you have made. Actually say each item to yourself and note your feelings.
b. Now read the list again, but with a slight difference. For each "can't," substitute the word "won't." For instance, "I can't say no to friends' requests" becomes "I won't say no." Circle any statements that are actually "won'ts."
c. Read the list for a third time. For this repetition substitute "I don't know how" for your original "can't." Instead of saying "I can't approach strangers," say, "I don't know how to approach strangers." *Correct* your original list to show which statements are truly "don't know hows."

After completing this exercise, you should be more aware of the power that negative self-fulfilling prophecies have on your self-concept and thus on your communication behavior. Imagine how differently you would behave if you eliminated any incorrect uses of the word "can't" from your thinking.

Harcourt Brace & Company

2.5 YOUR SELF-FULFILLING PROPHECIES

◆❖ Activity Type: Skill Builder

PURPOSES

1. To help you identify the self-fulfilling prophecies you impose on yourself.
2. To help you identify the self-fulfilling prophecies others impose on you.

INSTRUCTIONS

1. Identify three communication-related, self-fulfilling prophecies you impose on yourself. For each, identify the item, describe the prediction you make, and show how this prediction influences either your behavior or that of others.
2. Next, identify two communication-related, self-fulfilling prophecies others have imposed on you. For each, show how the other person's prediction affected your behavior.

PROPHECIES YOU IMPOSE ON YOURSELF

Example

Item *Inept in social situations*
Prediction *When I'm at a party or other social gathering, I think about how foolish I'll sound when I meet strangers.*
Outcome *I do sound foolish when I meet them. I stammer, avoid eye contact, and can't think of anything interesting to say.*
How your prediction affected outcome *I think that expecting to fail causes me to sound foolish. If I didn't expect to sound so foolish, I'd probably behave with more confidence.*

1. Item _____

   Prediction _____

   _____

   _____

   Outcome _____

   _____

   _____

   How prediction affected outcome _____

   _____

   _____

2. Item _____

Prediction _____

_____

_____

Outcome _____

_____

_____

How prediction affected outcome _____

_____

_____

3. Item _____

Prediction _____

_____

_____

Outcome _____

_____

_____

How prediction affected outcome _____

_____

_____

PROPHECIES OTHERS IMPOSE ON YOU

Example

Item *Good listener*
Prediction *My friends often share their problems with me and tell me that I'm a good listener.*
Outcome *I'm willing to listen in the future.*
How your prediction affected outcome *Being told I'm a good listener makes me more willing to lend an ear. If they told me I was no help, I'd probably discourage them from bringing me their problems in the future.*

1. Item _____

   Prediction _____

   _____

   _____

   Outcome _____

   _____

   _____

   How prediction affected outcome _____

   _____

   _____

2. Item _____

   Prediction _____

   _____

   _____

   Outcome _____

   _____

   _____

   How prediction affected outcome _____

   _____

   _____

Harcourt Brace & Company

2.6 SUCCESS IN MANAGING IDENTITIES

❖ Activity Type: Skill Builder

PURPOSES

1. To acknowledge at least one successful face that you have revealed to others.
2. To reflect on your level of self-monitoring in that instance.
3. To listen to the successful "faces" of others.

INSTRUCTIONS

1. In groups, describe to one another one instance in which each of you has successfully presented yourself to another person. Describe how you managed that identity of yourself. It may be a significant identity (you got a job you wanted or a date you wanted) or it may be an ongoing, slowly made success (you were a better parent this week or you kept your cool with your roommate during last week's conflict). Describe how you managed manner, setting and/or appearance to create the identity you wanted.
2. Describe to others how aware you were of your own behaviors. Describe whether you had high or low self-monitoring, and how effective or ineffective your level of monitoring was for the identity management situation.
3. Listen to the examples of others as you get to know people in your group.

THE SUCCESSFUL FACE I REVEALED TO OTHERS

_____

_____

_____

_____

HOW I MANAGED THE FACE:

Manner _____

_____

Setting _____

_____

Appearance _____

_____

Harcourt Brace & Company

EFFECTIVENESS OF SELF-MONITORING (LEVEL OF AWARENESS)

_____

_____

_____

_____

_____

IMPRESSIONS I RECEIVED FROM LISTENING TO OTHERS

_____

_____

_____

_____

_____

_____

_____

_____

_____

_____

_____

CROSSWORD PUZZLE

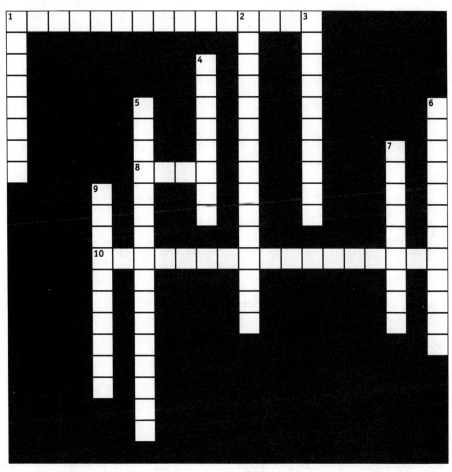

Across

1 the identity type that refers to a self-concept that is strongly "I" oriented, common in cultures where the main desire is to promote the self

8 the socially approved identity that a communicator tries to present

10 the tendency to look for people who confirm our self-concept

Down

1 the image one presents to others

2 the process of attending to one's behavior and using these observations to shape the way one behaves

3 the identity that refers to a self-concept that is highly dependent on belonging to a group, common in cultures where the main desire is to build connections between the self and others

4 information that was once true about the self but is no longer true

5 a prophecy that is a prediction or expectation of an event that makes the outcome more likely to occur than would otherwise have been the case

6 the relatively stable set of perceptions that each person holds of himself or herself

7 the self that refers to the person we believe ourselves to be in moments of candor

9 the self that refers to the image a person presents to others

TRUE/FALSE

Mark the statements below as true or false. Correct statements that are false on the lines below to create a true statement.

_____ **1.** Every aspect of your self-concept is equally important.

_____

_____ **2.** Most researchers agree that we are not born with a self-concept.

_____

_____ **3.** The influence of significant others becomes less powerful as we grow older.

_____

_____ **4.** People who dislike themselves are likely to believe that others won't like them either.

_____

_____ **5.** Research has shown that people with high self-esteem seek out partners who view them unfavorably because they are strong enough to take the criticism.

_____

_____ **6.** Luckily, your self-concept is not affected by the language that you speak.

_____

_____ **7.** In individualistic societies, there is a higher degree of communication apprehension.

_____

_____ **8.** The self-concept is such a powerful force on the personality that it not only determines how you see yourself in the present but also can actually influence your future behavior and that of others.

_____

_____ **9.** Research shows that people who believe they are incompetent are more likely than others to pursue rewarding relationships in an attempt to ally themselves with competent people.

_____

_____ **10.** The communication strategies we use to influence how others view us are all conscious behaviors.

_____

COMPLETION

Fill in the blanks below with the correct terms chosen from the list below.

distorted feedback obsolete information self-delusion
ego booster   ego buster   realistic expectations
realistic perceptions   manner   setting
appearance

1. _____ is someone who helps enhance your self-esteem by acting in ways that make you feel accepted, important and loved.

2. _____ is someone who acts to reduce your self-esteem.

3. _____ are messages that others send to you that are unrealistically positive or negative.

4. _____ consists of a communicator's words and nonverbal actions that help create a front.

5. _____ is information that was once true about you that is no longer true.

6. _____ are the personal items people use to shape an image.

7. _____ is the inability to see a real need for change in the self due to holding an unrealistically favorable picture of yourself.

8. _____ are reasonable goals to set for self-growth.

9. _____ refers to the physical items we use to influence how others view us.

10. _____ are relatively accurate views of the strengths and weaknesses of the self.

Harcourt Brace & Company

MULTIPLE CHOICE

Identify which principle influences the self-concept in each example. Place the letter of the correct term on the line adjacent to each description.

  a. obsolete information
  b. distorted feedback
  c. emphasis on perfection
  d. social expectations

_____ 1. You always scored more points than anyone else on your team in high school. You still think you're the best even though your college teammates are scoring more than you.

_____ 2. You keep getting down on yourself because you can't cook as well as Megan, even though you are a great student and a fair athlete.

_____ 3. You tell everyone how you "blew" the chemistry test and got a "C−" but you don't ever acknowledge your "A's" in math.

_____ 4. Your parents tell you, their friends, and all your relatives about all your wonderful accomplishments, even though you have only average achievement.

_____ 5. Janee says that you are insensitive to her perspective despite your many attempts to listen honestly to her and empathize.

_____ 6. You pay a lot of attention to the magazines showing perfectly dressed and groomed individuals and keep wishing you could look as good as they do.

_____ 7. You think of yourself as the shy fifth grader despite being at the social hub of at least three clubs on campus.

_____ 8. You feel uncomfortable accepting the compliments your friends honestly give you.

_____ 9. You're exhausted by trying to get all A's, work 30 hours a week, and be a loving romantic partner at the same time. You don't see how so many other people manage to get it all done.

_____ 10. "You're the perfect weight," your father tells you despite your recent gain of twenty pounds over the normal weight for your height.

Choose the *best* answer for each statement below:

11. Deciding which face–which part of you–to reveal is termed

    a. frontwork.
    b. identity management.
    c. hypocrisy.
    d. two-faced syndrome.

12. The most significant part of a person's self-concept

    a. is the social roles the person plays.
    b. is his or her appearance.
    c. is his or her accomplishments.
    d. will vary from person to person.

13. The self-concept begins

    a. at conception.
    b. in the womb.
    c. during the first year of life.
    d. at the onset of puberty.

14. Which of the following could be an example of a self-fulfilling prophecy?

    a. Sid is born with a very large nose.
    b. Marguerita has a very large, extended family.
    c. Serge is a Russian immigrant.
    d. Joy has given up on trying to talk to her unreasonable father.

15. The fact that none of us can see ourselves completely accurately illustrates the _____ nature of the self-concept.

    a. subjective
    b. objective
    c. unrealistic
    d. verification

Harcourt Brace & Company

STUDY GUIDE ANSWERS

CROSSWORD PUZZLE

Across:

1. individualistic
8. face
10. self-verification

Down (grid letters):

1. identity
2. self-monitoring
3. collective
4. obsolete
5. self-fulfilling
6. self-concept
7. perceived
9. presenting

TRUE/FALSE

1.	F	5.	F	9.	F
2.	T	6.	F	10.	F
3.	T	7.	F		
4.	T	8.	T		

Harcourt Brace & Company

COMPLETION

1. ego booster
2. ego buster
3. distorted feedback
4. manner
5. obsolete information
6. appearance
7. self-delusion
8. realistic expectations
9. setting
10. realistic perceptions

MULTIPLE CHOICE

1. a
2. c
3. d
4. b
5. b
6. c
7. a
8. d
9. c
10. b
11. b
12. d
13. c
14. d
15. a

Harcourt Brace & Company

Chapter 3

Perception: What You See Is What You Get

OUTLINE

Use this outline to take notes as you read the chapter in the text and/or as your instructor lectures in class.

I. The perception process

A. Selection
  1. Factors that influence selection
     a. Intense stimuli
     b. Repetitious stimuli
     c. Contrast or change in stimulation
     d. Motives
  2. Distortions in selection

B. Organization
  1. Figure–ground organization
  2. Perceptual schema
     a. Physical constructs
     b. Role constructs
     c. Interaction constructs
     d. Psychological constructs
     e. Membership constructs
  3. Effects of organization
     a. Forms impressions of others
     b. Affects the way we relate to others
     c. May lead to inaccurate generalizations
        1) Stereotyping
        2) Punctuation

C. Interpretation
  1. Relational satisfaction
  2. Degree of involvement with the other person
  3. Past experience
  4. Assumptions about human behavior
  5. Expectations
  6. Knowledge
  7. Self-concept

II. Influences on perception

A. Physiological
1. Senses
2. Age
3. Health
4. Fatigue
5. Hunger
6. Biological Cycles

B. Cultural Differences
1. Language translations
2. Value of talk
3. Nonverbal behaviors
4. Ethnicity
5. Geography

C. Social Roles

D. Gender Roles

E. Occupational Roles

F. Self-Concept
1. Judgments of others
2. Judgments of self

G. Shared Narratives

III. The accuracy—and inaccuracy—of perception

A. We Often Judge Ourselves More Charitably than Others

B. We Are Influenced by What Is Most Obvious

C. We Cling to First Impressions

D. We Tend to Assume Others Are Similar to Us

IV. Perception checking to prevent misunderstandings

A. Elements of Perception Checking
1. Describe behavior
2. Interpret behavior two ways
3. Request clarification

B. Perception-Checking Considerations
1. Completeness
2. Nonverbal congruency
3. Cultural rules
   a. Low-context cultures
   b. High-context cultures

Harcourt Brace & Company

V. Empathy and communication

    A. Empathy Defined

        1. Empathy–ability to re-create another's perspective

            a. Perspective taking

            b. Emotional dimension

            c. Genuine concern

        2. Sympathy–compassion for another's predicament

    B. The Pillow Method–A Tool for Building Empathy

        1. Position One: I'm right, you're wrong

        2. Position Two: You're right, I'm wrong

        3. Position Three: Both right, both wrong

        4. Position Four: The issue isn't as important as it seems

        5. Conclusion: There is truth in all four perspectives

KEY TERMS

Use these key terms to review major concepts from your text. Write the definition for each key term in the space to the right.

androgynous _____

attribution _____

cultural differences _____

empathy _____

figure–ground organization _____

gender roles _____

high-context culture _____

interaction constructs _____

interpretation _____

low-context culture _____

membership constructs _____

narrative _____

occupational roles _____

organization _____

Harcourt Brace & Company

perception _____

perception checking _____

perceptual schema _____

physical constructs _____

physiological influences _____

pillow method _____

psychological constructs _____

punctuation _____

role constructs _____

selection _____

self-serving bias _____

social roles _____

stereotyping _____

subcultural differences _____

sympathy _____

ACTIVITIES

3.1 GUARDING AGAINST PERCEPTUAL ERRORS

◆ Activity Type: Invitation to Insight

PURPOSES

1. To help you identify potentially distorted opinions you have formed about people.
2. To help you recognize some perceptual errors that may have contributed to those distorted opinions.

INSTRUCTIONS

1. Identify two people about whom you've formed strong opinions. These opinions can be positive or negative. In either case, describe them.
2. Using the checklist provided, comment on the accuracy or inaccuracy of your perceptions of each person. See Chapter 3 of *Looking Out/Looking In* for a more detailed description of the checklist factors. NOTE: Not every factor may apply to each person.
3. Record your conclusions at the end of the exercise.
4. Compare your examples with those of other classmates.

	EXAMPLE	PERSON A	PERSON B
Identify each person. Describe your opinions.	Joni is my wife's good friend. I don't like her; I think she's inconsiderate and selfish and boring. Her voice is shrill and I find her annoying.		
1. We are influenced by what is most obvious.	Because she is my wife's friend, Joni is around a lot, and it seems that I am always noticing her voice or her calls–perhaps I'm looking for them.		

Harcourt Brace & Company

	EXAMPLE	PERSON A	PERSON B
2. We cling to first impressions, even if wrong.	I haven't liked Joni from the beginning. She always used to call right at our dinnertime. Even though she doesn't do this anymore, I still remember it and I'm influenced by it.		
3. We tend to assume others are similar to us.			
4. We judge ourselves more charitably than others.	When Joni lost her job, I thought it was Joni's fault because she's so annoying Of course, when I got laid off a few months later, I complained heavily about the economy and knew being laid off had nothing to do with my performance or personality.		

CONCLUSIONS

Based on the observations above, how accurate or inaccurate are your perceptions of other people?

_____

_____

_____

_____

What might you do in the future to guard against inaccurate perceptions of people?

_____

_____

_____

_____

3.2 EXAMINING YOUR INTERPRETATIONS

◆ Activity Type: Invitation to Insight

PURPOSES

1. To help you identify the interpretations you make about others' behavior in your important interpersonal relationships.
2. To help you recognize the perceptual factors that influence those assumptions.
3. To help you consider the validity of your interpretations.

INTRODUCTION

There are many ways to interpret what another person says or does. For example, you may notice that a new classmate is wearing a cross necklace and imagine that she is a religious person, or you might notice that a friend isn't making much eye contact with you and assume that he is not telling you the truth.

We usually assume that our interpretations are accurate. In fact, these assumptions might be incorrect or quite different from how the other person sees himself or herself.

INSTRUCTIONS

1. For the next few days, observe three people and use the spaces below to record your interpretations of each.
2. After completing the information below, share your observations with each person involved and see if your interpretations match the explanations of each subject.

Example

Name *Stan Morris* _____ context *Neighbor and friend*

A. Describe an assumption about this person's thoughts or feelings.
   I've been thinking that Stan is mad at me, probably because I've been asking so many favors of him lately.

B. Describe at least two items of behavior (things the person has said or done) that lead you to believe your assumption about this person's thoughts or feelings is accurate.
   1. *When I asked to borrow his backpacking gear he said yes, but he mentioned several times how much it cost him.*
   2. *When I asked him for a ride to school last week when my car was in the shop, he said OK but didn't talk much and drove more quickly than usual.*

C. Give at least two reasons why your assumption about this person's thoughts or feelings may *not* be accurate. (You may ask the person you are observing for help.)
   1. *Stan is often a moody person. Even if he is upset, it may not be because of anything I've said or done.*

Harcourt Brace & Company

2. *I'm often hard on myself, taking the blame for anything that goes wrong. Perhaps I'm doing that here, and Stan doesn't mind doing me the favors.*

D. Which of the following factors influenced your perception of this person? Explain how each of these factors affected the accuracy or inaccuracy of your interpretations.

Physiological influences _____

_____

_____

Sex/occupational roles *Perhaps my being a woman has something to do with my self-doubt. I often wonder if I'm being too "forward" in asking a man for favors.*

Cultural/subcultural roles _____   _____

_____

_____

Self-concept *I often view myself as less desirable as a friend than other people I know. I think this leads me to interpret others' reactions as confirmations of my worst fears, whether or not those fears are valid.*

Person 1

Name _____   Context _____

A. Describe an assumption you have made about this person's thoughts or feelings.

_____

_____

_____

B. Describe at least two items of behavior (things the person has said or done) that lead you to believe your assumption about this person's thoughts or feelings is accurate.

1. _____

_____

_____

2. _____

_____

_____

_____

_____

C. Give at least two reasons why your assumption about this person's thoughts or feelings may not be accurate. (You may ask the person you are observing for help.)

1. _____

_____

_____

2. _____

_____

_____

_____

D. Which of the following factors influence your perception of this person? Explain how each of these factors affected the accuracy or inaccuracy of your interpretations.

Physiological influences _____

_____

_____

Sex/occupational roles _____

_____

_____

Cultural/subcultural roles _____

_____

_____

Harcourt Brace & Company

Self-concept _____

_____

_____

Person 2

    Name _____   Context _____

A. Describe an assumption you have made about this person's thoughts or feelings.

_____

_____

_____

B. Describe at least two items of behavior (things the person has said or done) that lead you to believe your assumption about this person's thoughts or feelings is accurate.

    1. _____

        _____

        _____

    2. _____

        _____

        _____

C. Give at least two reasons why your assumption about this person's thoughts or feelings may *not* be accurate. (You may ask the person you are observing for help.)

    1. _____

        _____

        _____

    2. _____

        _____

        _____

        _____

D. Which of the following factors influenced your perception of this person? Explain how each of these factors affected the accuracy or inaccuracy of your interpretations.

Physiological influences _____

_____

_____

Sex/occupational roles _____

_____

_____

Cultural/subcultural roles _____

_____

_____

Self-concept _____

_____

_____

Person 3

Name _____   Context _____

A. Describe an assumption you have made about this person's thoughts or feelings.

_____

_____

_____

B. Describe at least two items of behavior (things the person has said or done) that lead you to believe your assumption about this person's thoughts or feelings is accurate.

1. _____

_____

_____

Harcourt Brace & Company

2. _____

_____

_____

C. Give at least two reasons why your assumption about this person's thoughts or feelings may *not* be accurate. (You may ask the person you are observing for help.)

1. _____

_____

_____

2. _____

_____

_____

D. Which of the following factors influenced your perception of this person? Explain how each of these factors affected the accuracy or inaccuracy of your interpretations.

Physiological influences _____

_____

_____

Sex/occupational roles _____

_____

_____

Cultural/subcultural roles _____

_____

_____

Self-concept _____

_____

_____

Harcourt Brace & Company

3.3 SHIFTING PERSPECTIVES (PILLOW METHOD)

◆ Activity Type: Invitation to Insight

PURPOSES

1. To help you understand how others view an interpersonal issue.
2. To help you recognize the merits and drawbacks of each person's perspective.
3. To help you recognize how an interpersonal issue may not be as important as it first seems.

INSTRUCTIONS

1. Select one disagreement or other issue that is now affecting an interpersonal relationship.
2. Record enough background information for an outsider to understand the issue. Who is involved? How long has the disagreement been going on? What are the basic issues involved?
3. Describe the issue from each of the four positions listed below.
4. Record your conclusions at the end of this exercise.

Option

With a partner, role-play your situation orally, using 3.8 *Pillow Method.*

Background Information

_____

_____

_____

_____

_____

Position 1: Explain how you are right and the other person is wrong.

_____

_____

_____

_____

Position 2: Explain how the other person's position is correct, or at least understandable.

_____

_____

_____

_____

_____

_____

Position 3: Show that there are both correct (or understandable) and mistaken (or unreasonable) parts of both positions.

_____

_____

_____

_____

_____

_____

Position 4: Describe at least two ways in which the elements developed in positions 1–3 might affect your relationship. Describe at least one way in which the issue might be seen as *less* important than it was originally and describe at least one way in which the issue might be seen as *more* important than it was originally.

_____

_____

_____

_____

_____

_____

Harcourt Brace & Company

CONCLUSION

Explain how there is some truth in each of the preceding positions. Also explain how viewing the issue from each of the preceding positions has changed your perception of the issue and how it may change your behavior in the future. Explain how this issue and your understanding of it affect your relationship.

_____

_____

_____

_____

_____

3.4 OBSERVATION AND PERCEPTION

❖ Activity Type: Skill Builder

PURPOSES

1. To report your observations of another person clearly and accurately.
2. To report at least two interpretations about the meaning of your observations to another person.
3. To discuss and evaluate the various choices you have available to you when dealing with perceptual problems.

INSTRUCTIONS

1. As a group, detail three situations below in which there are potential perceptual problems.
2. Use the form below to record behavior for each relationship listed.
3. For each example of behavior, record two plausible interpretations.
4. Record a request for feedback.
5. With others in the group, rehearse how you could share with the person in question each example of behavior and the possible interpretations you have developed.
6. Evaluate the various other options you have to check out perceptions. Describe the probable outcome of each.

Example

Perceptual problem: *Jill's math professor is really annoying her–calling on her for answers and trying to get her involved more in the class. Jill is uncomfortable about this, but she is afraid that the professor might pay even more attention to her if she brings it up.*
Perception checking statement: *Professor Smith, I'm confused about something.*

> Behavior: *I've noticed that you call on me quite often–at least once each class, whether or not I raise my hand.*
> Interpretation A: *Sometimes I wonder if you're trying to catch me unprepared.*
> Interpretation B: *On the other hand, sometimes I think you're trying to challenge me by forcing me to keep on my toes.*
> Request for feedback: *Can you tell me why you call on me so often?*

Perception-checking options

1. *Jill could do nothing. Perhaps it would be better to wait and see if she has been imagining this by watching a bit more.*
2. *Jill could start initiating answers herself and see if Professor Smith changes behavior.*

Harcourt Brace & Company

3. *Jill could just tell the Prof that she doesn't like being called on. This might alienate her in the Prof's eyes, however, and might affect her grade.*
4. *Jill could just ask if the Prof was trying to embarrass her. We thought the Prof might not know what Jill was referring to, though, if she didn't describe behavior. The Prof probably teaches hundreds of students and might not realize what's going on in Jill's eyes.*
5. *Jill could do the complete perception-checking statement we wrote above. Our group thought this has a good chance for success if the Prof didn't get defensive. If Jill could deliver the statement in a non-defensive tone and then follow it up with how much she likes the class, perhaps the Prof would realize how much Jill is bothered.*

SITUATION ONE

Perceptual problem:_____

_____

_____

Perception-checking statement: _____

Behavior: _____

Interpretation A: _____

Interpretation B: _____

Request for feedback: _____

Perception-checking options:

_____

_____

_____

_____

_____

SITUATION TWO

Perceptual problem:_____

_____

_____

Perception-checking statement: _____

Behavior: _____

Interpretation A: _____

Interpretation B: _____

Request for feedback: _____

Perception-checking options:

_____

_____

_____

_____

_____

SITUATION THREE

Perceptual problem:_____

_____

_____

Perception-checking statement: _____

Behavior: _____

Interpretation A: _____

Interpretation B: _____

Request for feedback: _____

Perception-checking options:

_____

_____

_____

_____

_____

Harcourt Brace & Company

3.5 APPLYING PERCEPTION CHECKING

◆❖ Activity Type: Skill Builder

PURPOSE

To prepare, deliver, and evaluate effective perception-checking statements.

INSTRUCTIONS

1. Choose two people with whom you have relational concerns. Give careful consideration to the partners you choose, choose concerns that are real and important, and allow yourself enough time to discuss your concerns with each partner.
2. Identify the concern, its importance to you, and consider the best time and place to approach each person.
3. Prepare perception-checking statements to deliver to each person.
4. Deliver your perception statements, discussing with each person your understanding of his or her behavior and the accuracy or inaccuracy of your perceptions. OR discuss why you decided not to use perception checking in this situation—and what you did alternately.

PARTNER 1

Part One: Describe Your Concern

Partner's name_____

A. Describe your primary concern._____

_____

_____

B. Why is it important to you to clarify this matter? _____

_____

_____

C. When and where is the best time to talk with this person? _____

_____

_____

Part Two: Preparing Your Perception-Checking Statement

A.   Describe your observations of the other person's behavior._____

_____

_____

B.   Write one interpretation that you believe could explain the behaviors you have observed.

_____

_____

_____

C.   Now write a second interpretation that is distinctly different from your previous one and which you believe could also explain the behavior you have observed.

_____

_____

_____

D.   Make a request for feedback. _____

Part Three: Sharing Your Perception-Checking Statement

Meet with your partner and (1) share your description of this person's behavior, (2) explain both of your interpretations of the behavior, and (3) ask your partner to react to the interpretations you have shared.

Describe the outcome of your conversation with your partner. _____

_____

_____

_____

or, if you think perception checking would not be appropriate or effective, explain why you decided not to use perception checking in this situation–and what you did instead.

_____

_____

_____

Harcourt Brace & Company

PARTNER 2

Part One: Describe Your Concern

Partner's name_____

   A.   Describe your primary concern._____

   _____

   _____

   B.   Why is it important to you to clarify this matter? _____

   _____

   _____

   C.   When and where is the best time to talk with this person? _____

   _____

   _____

Part Two: Preparing your Perception-Checking Statement

   A.   Describe your observations of the other person's behavior._____

   _____

   _____

   B.   Write one interpretation that you believe could explain the behaviors you have
        observed.

   _____

   _____

   _____

   C.   Now write a second interpretation which is distinctly different from your previous
        one and which you believe could also explain the behavior you have observed.

   _____

   _____

   _____

Harcourt Brace & Company

D. Make a request for feedback. _____

Part Three: Sharing Your Perception-Checking Statement

Meet with your partner and (1) share your description of this person's behavior, (2) explain both of your interpretations of the behavior, and (3) ask your partner to react to the interpretations you have shared.

Describe the outcome of your conversation with your partner. _____

_____

_____

_____

OR, if you think perception checking would not be appropriate or effective, explain why you decided not to use perception checking in this situation—and what you did instead.

_____

_____

_____

SUMMARY

1. How accurate were your interpretations in the two situations above?

    _____

    _____

    _____

2. Based on your experiences in this exercise, in what circumstances are your interpretations accurate? When are they likely to be inaccurate? Consider the people involved, the topic of communication, and your personal moods and thoughts.

    _____

    _____

    _____

    _____

Harcourt Brace & Company

3. How did your partners react when you communicated by using perception checking? How did these reactions differ from the reactions you get when you jump to conclusions instead of using perception checking? If you decided not to use perception checking, what did you do instead and what were the results? How could this improve your relationships in the future?

_____

_____

_____

_____

4. Based on your experience in this exercise, when and how can you use perception checking in your everyday communication? With whom? In what situations? What difference will using perception checking make in your interpersonal relationships?

_____

_____

_____

_____

Harcourt Brace & Company

3.6 PERCEPTION-CHECKING PRACTICE

❖ Activity Type: Skill Builder

PURPOSE

To create effective perception-checking statements.

INSTRUCTIONS

Option A:

Practice writing perception-checking statements for items 1–10 below.

Option B:

1. Join with a partner to create a dyad. Label one person A and the other B.
2. Both A and B should write perception-checking statements for items 1–10 below.
3. A then delivers items 1–5 to B orally. B should use Evaluation Form 3.7 to rate A's responses for these items.
4. B delivers items 6–10 orally to A. A should use Checklist 3.7 to rate B's responses for these items.

Option C:

Practice items 1–10 below orally with a partner. Deliver your best perception check in class while your instructor evaluates you.

Example

Yesterday you saw your friend walking on the beach engaged in what looked to you like an intense conversation with your recent date, Chris.

Perception-checking statement *When I saw you yesterday walking on the beach with Chris, I didn't know what to make of it. I thought you might be talking about that class you're taking together, but I also wondered whether you're interested in dating Chris. Are you interested in Chris as a friend, or as a date?*

1. During last week's exam you thought you saw your friend Jim, who sits next to you in class, looking at your paper.

_____

_____

_____

2. Ever since the school year began, members of your family have made a point of asking how you are doing several times each month. They have just asked again.

_____

_____

_____

3. Your friend Carlo was driving you home from a party last night when he began to weave the car between lanes on the highway. You were uncomfortable, but didn't say anything then. Now it is the next morning and Carlo shows up to take you to a class. You have decided to bring up the incident.

_____

_____

_____

4. It seems that every time you have been leaving your house lately, your roommate runs after you, asking for a ride somewhere. Your roommate has a car, but you haven't seen it lately. You are in a hurry now, and your roommate has just asked for another ride.

_____

_____

_____

5. You return home at night to find your roommate, Tom, reading on the couch. When you walk into the room and greet Tom, he grunts and turns his face away from you and keeps reading.

_____

_____

_____

6. Last week your instructor, Dr. Green, returned your exam with a low grade and the comment, "This kind of work paints a bleak picture for the future." You have approached him to discuss the remark.

_____

_____

_____

7. In one of your regular long-distance phone conversations you ask your favorite cousin, Mike, about the state of his up-and-down romantic life. He sighs and says, "Oh, it's OK, I guess."

_____

_____

_____

8. Your girlfriend or boyfriend (or spouse) announces that she or he plans to spend next Friday night with friends from work. You usually spend Friday nights alone together.

_____

_____

_____

9. Last week your supervisor at work, Ms. White, gave you a big assignment. Three times since then she has asked you whether you're having any trouble with it.

_____

_____

_____

10. Last weekend your next-door neighbor, Steve, raked a big pile of leaves near your property line, promising to clean them up after work on Monday. It's Wednesday, and the wind is blowing the leaves into your yard.

_____

_____

_____

11. One of your classmates sits by you every day in class and runs after you to walk across campus; now he has started calling you at home every evening. He now suggests that you do some things on the weekend together.

_____

_____

_____

Harcourt Brace & Company

12. You've noticed one of your office mates looking over at you a number of times during the past few days. At first she looked away quickly, but now she smiles every time you look up and catch her looking at you. You've been under a lot of pressure at work lately and have been extremely busy. You can't understand why she keeps looking at you. You've decided to ask.

_____

_____

_____

3.7 PERCEPTION CHECKING

❖ Activity Type: Oral Skill

PURPOSE

To evaluate your skill at using perception-checking statements.

INSTRUCTIONS

1. Identify a situation in your life in which a perception check might be appropriate. Describe the situation to the person who will be evaluating your skill check.
2. Deliver a complete perception check to your evaluator, without using notes, following the criteria listed in Chapter 3 of *Looking Out/Looking In* and outlined in the checklist below.
3. Describe below (or on a separate page)

   a. how well perception checking might (or might not) work in the situation you have chosen. If you do not think a complete perception check is the best approach for this situation, explain why and describe a more promising alternative.

   b. the degree to which you could (or could not) increase your communicative competence by using perception checks in other situations.

CHECKLIST

_____   Describes background for potential perception-checking situation.

_____   Delivers complete perception check

        _____   Reports at least one behavior that describes what the person has said or done.

        _____   States two interpretations that are distinctly different, equally probable, and are based on the reported behavior.

        _____   Makes a sincere request for feedback clarifying how to interpret the reported behavior.

_____   Verbal and nonverbal behavior

        _____   Reflects sincere desire for clarification of the perception.

        _____   Sounds realistic and consistent with style of the speaker.

        _____   Uses nonthreatening, nondefensive voice and eye contact.

Harcourt Brace & Company

_____ Realistically and clearly assesses how perception checking and other alternatives can be used in everyday life.

_____ In situation described here.

_____ In other situations (be specific).

3. a. How well might perception-checking work in this situation?

    _____

    _____

    _____

    _____

    _____

    b. How could you increase your competence by using perception-checking in other situations?

    _____

    _____

    _____

    _____

    _____

Harcourt Brace & Company

NAME _____

3.8 PILLOW METHOD

◆❖ Activity Type: Oral Skill

PURPOSE

To use the Pillow Method to illustrate understanding of multiple perspectives on a given issue.

INSTRUCTIONS

1. Use the material from *3.3 Shifting Perspectives (Pillow Method)* to share each position from the "Pillow Method" with either the real-life person involved in this issue or a classmate.
2. Invite your partner to correct you if you have misunderstood his or her position, or ask a classmate to role-play your partner, interrupting you if she or he thinks another aspect of the issue has been neglected. Use perception checking, as necessary, to clarify perceptions with your partner.
3. Based on your experience in this skill check, describe how you could integrate the Pillow Method into your relationships.

CHECKLIST

5 = superior   4 = excellent   3 = good   2 = fair   1 = poor

Engages in appropriate nonverbal behavior
  −looks at partner
  −speaks in nondefensive tone
  −faces partner

Presents relevant background information _____

Explains Position 1 (I'm right; other person is wrong) _____

Explains Position 2 (partner is correct/understandable) _____

Explains Position 3 (both positions are correct/mistaken−even partly) _____

Explains Position 4 (effects on relationship) _____

Uses perception checking as necessary _____

Presents conclusion _____

Describes how Pillow Method could be applied to personal relationships _____

Total _____

CROSSWORD PUZZLE

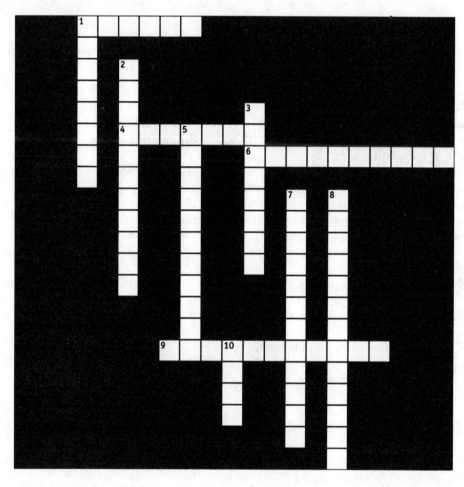

Across

1 a method which examines the four sides and middle of a perceptual issue
4 the ability to project oneself into another person's point of view, so as to experience the other's thoughts and feelings
6 constructs that are perceptual schema that categorize people according to the groups to which they belong
9 possessing both masculine and feminine traits

Down

1 constructs that are perceptual schema that categorize people according to their appearances
2 constructs that are perceptual schema that categorize people according to their social behaviors
3 compassion for another's situation
5 the process of attaching meaning to behavior
7 exaggerated generalizations associated with a categorizing system
8 constructs that are perceptual schema that categorize people according to their apparent personalities
10 constructs that are perceptual schema that categorize people according to their social positions

Harcourt Brace & Company

TRUE/FALSE

Mark the statements below as true or false. Correct statements that are false on the lines below to create a true statement.

_____ 1. Since we are able to perceive with our senses, our perceptions make us aware of all that is going on around us.

_____

_____ 2. Selection, organization, and interpretation comprise the three steps of the perception process.

_____

_____ 3. The fact that we pay attention to some things and ignore others illustrates the fact that selection is an objective process.

_____

_____ 4. Perceptual schema are cognitive frameworks that allow us to classify or organize the information we get about others.

_____

_____ 5. It is wrong to generalize about anybody or any group, even if the generalizations are accurate.

_____

_____ 6. We sometimes view people more favorably if we have a relationship with them.

_____

_____ 7. Adrenal and sex hormones affect the way both men and women relate to each other.

_____

_____ 8. All cultures view talk as desirable, using it for social purposes as well as to perform tasks.

_____

_____ 9. Within the boundaries of a country, most perceptions are similar.

_____

Harcourt Brace & Company

_____ **10.** People with high self-esteem are more likely to think highly of themselves, and thus more likely to have a poor opinion of others.

COMPLETION

Fill in the blanks below with the correct terms chosen from the list below.

membership constructs   physical constructs   sympathy
interaction constructs   perceptual schema   empathy
psychological constructs   role constructs   stereotypes
androgynous

1. _____ are the cognitive frameworks that allow individuals to organize perceptual data that they have selected from the environment.

There are five different ways that we organize these frameworks:

2. _____ are perceptual schema that categorize people according to their social position.

3. _____ are perceptual schema that categorize people according to their appearance.

4. _____ are perceptual schema that categorize people according to their apparent personalities.

5. _____ are perceptual schema that categorize people according to their social behavior.

6. _____ are perceptual schema that categorize people according to the groups to which they belong.

7. _____ is the ability to re-create another person's perspective.

8. _____ is feeling compassion for another person's predicament.

9. _____ are exaggerated beliefs associated with a categorizing system.

10. _____ is an example of a psychological sex type that influences perception.

MULTIPLE CHOICE

RECOGNIZING PERCEPTION-CHECKING ELEMENTS

For each of the following statements, identify which element of the perception-checking statement is missing. Place the letter of the most accurate evaluation of the statement on the line before the statement.

a. This statement doesn't describe behavior.
b. This statement doesn't give two distinctly different interpretations.
c. This statement neglects to request clarification of the perception.
d. There is nothing missing from this perception-checking statement.

_____ **1.** "Why did you send me those flowers? Is this a special occasion or what?"

_____ **2.** "When you went straight to bed when you came home, I thought you were sick. Are you all right?"

_____ **3.** "You must be either really excited about your grades or anxious to talk about something important. What's going on?"

_____ **4.** "When you ran out smiling, I figured you were glad to see me and ready to go, or maybe you were having such a good time here you wanted to stay longer."

_____ **5.** "I thought you were angry with me when you didn't come over this afternoon like you'd said you would. But then I thought maybe something came up at work. What is it?"

_____ **6.** "When you told me you expected to get an outline with my report, I thought you were trying to trick me into doing more work, or maybe you didn't realize that wasn't part of my job."

_____ **7.** "When you told everyone my parents own the company, you must have been indicating I was hired here only because of them. Is that what you think?"

_____ **8.** "When you passed the ball to me, I thought you wanted me to shoot. Did you?"

_____ **9.** "Why is it that you're so pleased with yourself? Did you win the lottery or accomplish something great? What's up?"

_____ **10.** "Dad, when you told my friend Art what a great athlete you think I am, I thought you were either really proud of me and wanted to brag a little, or maybe you wanted to see what Art and I had in common by the way he responded. What were you up to?"

Harcourt Brace & Company

STUDY GUIDE ANSWERS

CROSSWORD PUZZLE

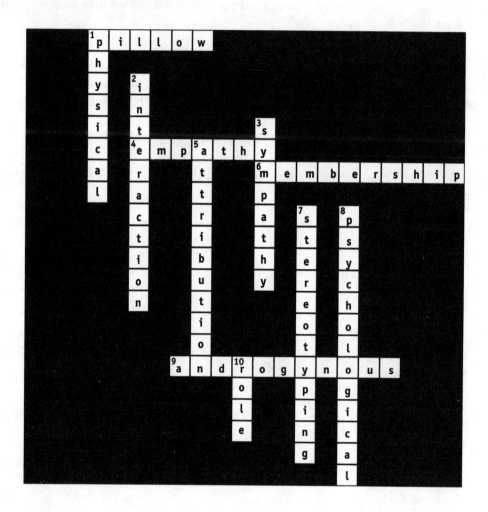

TRUE/FALSE

1. F	3. F	5. F	7. T	9. F
2. T	4. T	6. T	8. F	10. F

Harcourt Brace & Company

COMPLETION

1. perceptual schema
2. role constructs
3. physical constructs
4. psychological constructs
5. interaction constructs
6. membership constructs
7. empathy
8. sympathy
9. stereotypes
10. androgynous

MULTIPLE CHOICE

1. b
2. b
3. a
4. c
5. d
6. c
7. b
8. b
9. a
10. d

Harcourt Brace & Company

Chapter 4   Emotions

OUTLINE

Use this outline to take notes as you read the chapter in the text and/or as your instructor lectures in class.

I. What are emotions?

A. Physiological Changes

B. Nonverbal Reactions

C. Cognitive Interpretations

II. Types of emotions

A. Primary and Mixed

B. Intense and Mild

III. Influences on emotional expression

A. Culture

B. Gender

C. Social Conventions

D. Social Roles

E. Emotional Contagion

F. Fear of Self-Disclosure

IV. Guidelines for expressing emotions

A. Recognize feelings

B. Think about how to describe feelings
   1. Avoid emotional counterfeits
   2. Express verbally
      a. Use single words
      b. Describe what's happening to you
      c. Describe what you'd like to do
   3. Avoid discounting feelings
   4. Avoid coded feelings
   5. Focus on a specific set of circumstances

C. Share multiple feelings

D. Recognize difference between feelings, talking and acting

E. **Accept responsibility for your feelings**

F. **Consider when and where to express your feelings**

V. Managing difficult emotions

A. **Facilitative and Debilitative Emotions**
   1. Intensity
   2. Duration

B. **Thoughts Cause Feelings**

C. **Irrational Thinking and Debilitative Emotions**
   1. Fallacy of perfection
   2. Fallacy of approval
   3. Fallacy of shoulds
   4. Fallacy of overgeneralization
      a. Limited amount of evidence
      b. Exaggerated shortcomings
      c. Abuse of the verb "to be"
   5. Fallacy of causation
      a. Believe you cause emotions/pain for others
         1) Fail to have your own needs met
         2) Begin resenting others
         3) Others can't trust you
      b. Believe others cause your emotions
   6. Fallacy of helplessness
   7. Fallacy of catastrophic expectations

D. **Minimizing Debilitative Emotions**
   1. Monitor your emotional reactions
   2. Note the activating event
   3. Record your self-talk
   4. Dispute your irrational beliefs

KEY TERMS

Use these key terms to review major concepts from your text. Write the definition for each key term in the space to the right.

activating event_____

cognitive interpretations_____

debilitative emotions _____

duration _____

emotional contagion _____

Harcourt Brace & Company

emotional counterfeits _____

emotions _____

facilitative emotions _____

fallacy of approval _____

fallacy of catastrophic expectations _____

fallacy of causation _____

fallacy of helplessness _____

fallacy of overgeneralization _____

fallacy of perfection _____

fallacy of shoulds _____

intensity _____

irrational fallacies _____

mixed emotions _____

nonverbal reactions _____

physiological changes _____

Plutchik's "emotion wheel" _____

primary emotions _____

proprioceptive stimuli _____

rational–emotive therapy _____

self-talk _____

Harcourt Brace & Company

ACTIVITIES

4.1 THE COMPONENTS OF EMOTION

❖ Activity Type: Skill Builder

PURPOSE

To help you identify the components of emotion.

INSTRUCTIONS

1. In groups, read each of the situations described below and describe how the emotions you would experience might manifest themselves in each of the components listed. Compare the responses of group members.
2. After finishing the examples provided for you, record 3 examples of your own here (include the incident, the emotion(s), physiological changes, nonverbal reactions, and cognitive interpretations):

1. _____

_____

_____

_____

2. _____

_____

_____

_____

3. _____

_____

_____

_____

INCIDENT	EMOTION(S)	PHYSIOLOGICAL CHANGES	NONVERBAL REACTIONS	COGNITIVE INTERPRETATION (THOUGHTS)
Example You've been assigned to deliver an oral presentation in one of your classes. It's now time to give your speech.	nervousness	pounding heart, churning stomach.	quavery voice, slightly trembling hands	"I hope, I don't make a fool of myself."
1. You're out on the town with friends for the evening. A companion asks you to dance.				
2. You're out on the town with friends for the evening. A companion asks you to chat.				
3. You're telling a joke or story. Just as you reach the punch line, you notice your listener stifle a yawn.				
4. At the beginning of class, one of your professors says, "I'd like to talk to you in my office after the lecture."				

Harcourt Brace & Company

4.2 FIND THE FEELINGS

❖ Activity Type: Skill Builder

PURPOSES

1. To help you distinguish true feeling statements from counterfeit expressions of emotion.
2. To increase your ability to express your feelings clearly.

INSTRUCTIONS

1. In groups, identify the true feeling statements below.
2. Analyze the statements for accuracy of feeling (check your analysis at the end of this exercise).
3. Rewrite statements that do not clearly or accurately express the speaker's feelings. (HINT: Statements that could be prefaced with "I think" are not always expressions of emotions. If the statements could be preceded by "I am," there is a good likelihood that they express feelings.)
4. Record examples of your own at the end of the exercise.

Example

That's the most disgusting thing I've ever heard!
Analysis *This isn't a satisfactory statement, since the speaker isn't clearly claiming that he or she is disgusted.*
Restatement *I'm upset and angry that those parents left their young children alone overnight.*

1. You're being awfully sensitive about that.

   Analysis_____

   _____

   Restatement _____

   _____

2. I can't figure out how to approach him.

   Analysis_____

   Restatement _____

   _____

3. I'm confused about what you want from me.

Analysis _____

Restatement _____

_____

4. I feel as if you're trying to hurt me.

Analysis _____

Restatement _____

_____

5. It's hopeless!

Analysis _____

Restatement _____

_____

6. I don't know how to tell you this . . .

Analysis _____

Restatement _____

_____

7. What's bothering you?

Analysis _____

Restatement _____

_____

8. I feel like the rug's been pulled out from under me.

Analysis _____

Restatement _____

_____

9. I feel like I've been stabbed in the back.

Analysis_____

Restatement_____

_____

10. You're so pathetic.

Analysis_____

Restatement_____

Now record three feeling statements of your own. Analyze and, if necessary, restate.

1. _____.

Analysis_____

Restatement_____

_____

2. _____.

Analysis_____

Restatement_____

_____

3. _____.

Analysis_____

Restatement_____

_____

Answers to "4.2 Find the Feelings"

1. The speaker here is labeling another's feelings, but saying nothing about his or her own. Is the speaker concerned, irritated, or indifferent to the other person's suspected sensitivity? We don't know. Possible restate: "I'm worried that I teased you too much about your hair."

2. The emotion here is implied but not stated. The speaker might be frustrated, perplexed, or tired. Possible restate: "I'm unsure about telling him the truth about my absence."

Harcourt Brace & Company

3. Here is a clear statement of the speaker's emotional state. Possible restate: "I'm confused about whether you want me to pay cash or charge it."
4. Just because we say "I feel" doesn't mean a feeling is being expressed. This is an interpretation statement. Possible restate: "I'm anxious about trusting you after you lied to me last week."
5. How does the speaker feel about the hopeless situation: resigned, sad, desperate? We haven't been told. Possible restate: "I feel frustrated after failing three math quizzes in a row.
6. Again, no feeling stated. Is the speaker worried, afraid, distraught? Possible restate: "I'm hesitant to tell you about my plans for summer."
7. This could be a statement of concern, irritation, or genuine confusion. Nonverbal clues can help us decide, but a feeling statement would tell us for certain. Possible restate: "I'm concerned that I may have offended you in some way."
8. Here's a metaphorical statement of feeling, strongly suggesting surprise or shock. This sort of message probably does an adequate job of expressing the emotion here, but it might be too vague for some people to understand. Possible restate: "I feel insecure right now since I didn't get the job I was expecting."
9. This is another metaphorical statement of feeling, strongly suggesting hurt or betrayal. While this statement may do an adequate job of expressing the emotion, it might be misinterpreted by some people, and it might be too strong a statement for the actual situation. Possible restate: "I'm hurt that Joe told you what I said in confidence."
10. This is the speaker's interpretation of someone else's behavior. It contains no feeling. Possible restate: "I'm irritated that you say you're tired and overworked when I've just worked a week of 10-hour shifts."

Harcourt Brace & Company

4.3 STATING EMOTIONS EFFECTIVELY

❖ Activity Type: Skill Builder

PURPOSE

To help you express the emotions you experience clearly and appropriately.

INSTRUCTIONS

1. Identify what's ineffective or unclear about each of the following feeling statements.
2. Rewrite the feeling statements making them more effective. Use the following guidelines for sharing feelings:
    Recognize feelings
    Describe feelings (concise, not discounted, not coded, focused on specifics)
    Share multiple feelings
    Differentiate between feeling , talking and acting
    Accept responsibility for your feelings
    Consider when and where to express

FEELING STATEMENT	IDENTIFY INEFFECTIVE, UNCLEAR ELEMENTS/REWRITE STATEMENT
Example When you complimented me in front of everyone at the party, I was really embarrassed.	I didn't express the mixed emotions I was feeling. I could have expressed this better by saying "When you complimented me at the party, I was glad you were proud of me, but I was embarrassed that you did it in front of so many people."
1. You make me so mad.	
2. I can't believe you act like that– I don't want to see you anymore.	
3. I don't care if you are rushed. We have to settle this now.	

FEELING STATEMENT	IDENTIFY INEFFECTIVE, UNCLEAR ELEMENTS/REWRITE STATEMENT
4. I was a little ticked off when you didn't show up.	
5. You're always criticizing me.	
6. Sure would be nice if people expressed appreciation.	
7. You jerk—you forgot to put gas in the car.	
8. It's about time you paid up.	
9. You're the best! Thanks for everything.	
10. I feel like a heel.	
11. I guess I'm a little attracted to him.	
12. She sends me into outer space.	

Harcourt Brace & Company

4.4 SELF-TALK

❖ Activity Type: Skill Builder

PURPOSES

1. To discover the self-talk in many common statements.
2. To identify any fallacies in self-talk.
3. To dispute any irrational self-talk.

INSTRUCTIONS

1. In groups, analyze the statements below.
2. Expand the self-talk behind each statement by using details from your personal experience to help discover things people think but often do not admit.
3. Identify any fallacies contained in the self-talk:

   approval   overgeneralization
   perfection   helplessness
   shoulds   catastrophic expectations
   causation

4. Dispute any irrational self-talk.

STATEMENT	SELF-TALK	FALLACIES	DISPUTE ANY FALLACIES
Example: He's too moody.	I can't stand his moodiness. He always acts depressed. I can never make him happy.	Overgeneralization, Causation, Helplessness	If I couldn't stand his moodiness, I would leave. He doesn't always act depressed. It is just that I get upset when I can't help him. It is not my responsibility to make him happy. I'll do what I can but not expect myself to solve all his problems.
1. I don't know why I even bother to study for her stupid tests.			

Harcourt Brace & Company

STATEMENT	SELF-TALK	FALLACIES	DISPUTE ANY FALLACIES
2. I never get any credit for trying around here.			
3. This place is unbearable with him around.			
4. He is so embarrassing because he has no manners.			
5. If I bring it up, we will fight.			
6. I hate him!			
7. I can't believe you told me to buy this stupid car.			
8. This guy is a total jerk.			

STATEMENT	SELF-TALK	FALLACIES	DISPUTE ANY FALLACIES
9. She's just like her mother.			
10. He's the perfect man. I'll be totally happy forever.			
11. I'll never get out of here because I can't make her stop talking.			
12. She thinks she's so gorgeous.			

As a group, identify the most common examples of your own self-talk, the fallacies involved, and the disputing you need to do to keep emotionally healthy.

STATEMENT	SELF-TALK	FALLACIES	DISPUTE ANY FALLACIES
1.			
2.			

STATEMENT	SELF-TALK	FALLACIES	DISPUTE ANY FALLACIES
3.			
4.			
5.			

4.5 DISPUTING IRRATIONAL THOUGHTS

◆ Activity Type: Invitation to Insight

PURPOSE

To help you minimize debilitative emotions by eliminating irrational thinking.

INSTRUCTIONS

1. Use the chart opposite to record incidents in which you experience communication-related debilitative emotions. The incidents needn't involve overwhelming feelings: mildly debilitative emotions are appropriate for consideration as well.
2. For each incident (activating event), record the self-talk that leads to the emotion you experienced.
3. If the self-talk you've identified is based on any of the irrational fallacies described in *Looking Out/Looking In*, identify them.
4. In each case where irrational thinking exists, dispute the irrational fallacies and provide an alternative, more rational interpretation of the event.
5. After completing the examples, record your conclusions here (or put them on a separate page):

CONCLUSIONS

1. What are the situations in which you often experience debilitative emotions?

   _____

   _____

2. What irrational beliefs do you subscribe to most often? Label them and explain.

   _____

   _____

   _____

3. How can you think more rationally to reduce the number and intensity of irrational emotions? (Give specific examples related to other aspects of your life, as well as referring to the activating events you have described in this exercise.)

   _____

   _____

   _____

   _____

Harcourt Brace & Company

ACTIVATING EVENT	SELF-TALK	BASED ON ANY IRRATIONAL FALLACIES?	EMOTION(S)	DISPUTE IRRATIONAL THINKING AND PROVIDE ALTERNATIVE INTERPRETATION
Example getting ready for job interview	"The employer will probably ask me a question I can't answer. I'll probably blow the interview. I'll never get a good job–it's hopeless!"	catastrophic failure overgeneralization helplessness	apprehension	There's certainly a *chance* that I'll blow the interview, but there's at least as good a chance that I'll do all right. I'm going overboard when I tell myself that there's no hope. The smartest idea is to do my best and not create a self-fulfilling prophecy of failing.
1.				
2.				
3.				
4.				
5.				

CROSSWORD PUZZLE

Across

4 emotions that prevent a person from functioning effectively
5 basic emotions
6 the strength of an emotion
8 a fallacy of thinking that believes that acceptance is needed from others
9 interpretations that are the thoughts that accompany strong emotions
11 changes that are the body's internal physical response to strong emotions
12 reactions that are the visible physical signs in response to strong emotions

Down

1 the nonvocal process of thinking
2 emotions that are combinations of primary emotions
3 emotions that contribute to effective functioning
5 stimuli that are sensations activated by movement of internal tissues
7 a fallacy of thinking that believes that no errors should be made in communication performance
10 the length of an emotion

TRUE/FALSE

Mark the statements below as true or false. Correct statements that are false on the lines below to create a true statement.

_____ **1.** According to Zimbardo's survey of shyness, people who labeled themselves "not shy" behaved in virtually the same way as those people who labeled themselves "shy" in certain social situations.

_____

_____ **2.** Women consistently score higher than men on the PONS test, which measures the ability to recognize emotions that are expressed in the facial expressions, movements, and vocal cues of others.

_____

_____ **3.** In opposite-sex twosomes, research shows that the woman is almost always better at interpreting the man's nonverbal signals than the man is at interpreting the woman's.

_____

_____ **4.** In mainstream North American society, the unwritten rules of communication encourage the direct expression of most emotions.

_____

_____ **5.** "I feel confined" is an emotional counterfeit statement.

_____

_____ **6.** Using many words to express a feeling is better than just summarizing feelings in a few words.

_____

_____ **7.** A certain amount of negative emotion can be constructive or facilitative.

_____

_____ **8.** It's the interpretations people make of events that cause their feelings.

_____

Harcourt Brace & Company

_____ **9.** Subscribing to the myth of perfection may diminish your own self-esteem, but it won't keep others from liking you.

_____

_____ **10.** The rational-emotive approach to emotions is nothing more than trying to talk yourself out of feeling bad.

_____

COMPLETION

Fill in the blanks below with the correct terms chosen from the list below.

catastrophic expectations   helplessness   causation
overgeneralization   shoulds   approval
perfection   activating event   monitoring
disputing

1. _____ is an irrational fallacy that operates on the assumption that if something bad can possibly happen, it will.

2. _____ is an irrational fallacy that suggests that satisfaction in life is determined by forces beyond your control.

3. _____ is an irrational fallacy based on the belief that emotions are the result of other people and things rather than one's own self-talk.

4. _____ is an irrational fallacy that makes a broad claim based on a limited amount of evidence.

5. _____ is an irrational fallacy based on the inability to distinguish between what is and what ought to be.

6. _____ is an irrational fallacy in which people go to incredible lengths to seek acceptance from virtually everyone.

7. _____ is an irrational fallacy in which people believe that worthwhile communicators should be able to handle every situation with complete confidence and skill.

8. _____ is the single large incident or series of small incidents that lead to thoughts or beliefs about the incident.

9. _____ is the process of recognizing the physiological, nonverbal, and cognitive components of emotions.

10. _____ is the process of recognizing mistaken thinking and developing alternative thinking.

MULTIPLE CHOICE

Choose the letter of the irrational fallacy contained in the self-talk found below.

a. perfection
b. approval
c. shoulds
d. overgeneralization

e. causation
f. helplessness
g. catastrophic expectations

_____ 1. "If only I didn't put my foot in my mouth when I ask someone out."

_____ 2. "I just can't initiate conversations—that's all there is to it."

_____ 3. "He shouldn't be off with his friends on Friday night."

_____ 4. "If she doesn't like this shirt, I'll be so upset."

_____ 5. "There was a major fire the last time we left; there will probably be an earthquake this time."

_____ 6. "He's never romantic."

_____ 7. "She's a cold fish; I'm lucky if I get a kiss."

_____ 8. "You ought to drink less."

_____ 9. "You're going to die going to Mexico at spring break."

_____ 10. "I've had a class in interpersonal communication; I can't believe I insulted her just now."

_____ 11. "Shaw makes me so mad with all his great grades."

_____ 12. "She'll be devastated if I break up with her."

_____ 13. "It's not even worth trying to reach him."

_____ 14. "I hope they don't notice how much weight I've gained."

Choose the best answer for each of the statements below.

15. Which of the following statements about emotions and culture is true?

    a. The same events will generate the same emotions in all cultures.
    b. Certain basic emotions are experienced by all people around the world.
    c. People from different cultures express happiness and sadness with facial difference.
    d. Fear of strangers is as strong in Japan as it is in the U.S.

16. Which of the following statements about gender and emotion is true?

    a. Women and men are equally likely to express feelings of vulnerability.
    b. Men and women are equally good at recognizing the emotions of others.
    c. Men are less bashful about revealing their strengths and positive emotions than women are.
    d. The stereotypical female notion of emotional expressiveness is superior to that of the stereotypical male.

17. All of the following statements about social emotion are true *except:*

    a. Genuine emotional expressions are rare.
    b. The emotions that people do share directly are usually positive.
    c. Married couples disclose positive and negative feelings about absent third parties.
    d. Married couples disclose hostility feelings regularly.

18. Which of the following is a true feeling statement?

    a. "I feel like watching a movie."
    b. "I feel like you're lonely."
    c. "I'm irritated by the ticking clock."
    d. "I'm totally involved."

19. Which of the following *best* improves the expression of emotion in the statement "I feel like giving up"?

    a. "I'm frustrated after asking him to pay his telephone bill three times."
    b. "I'm going to kill him."
    c. "I am going to tell the landlord about this frustrating situation."
    d. "I feel he's been unreasonable."

20. How could you improve your emotional expression in the statement "She makes me so totally upset, always thinking she is better than everyone else."

    a. Take out the "totally."
    b. Focus on a specific set of circumstances.
    c. Accept responsibility for your feelings.
    d. All of the above could improve the statement.
    e. The statement is fine the way it is.

CROSSWORD PUZZLE

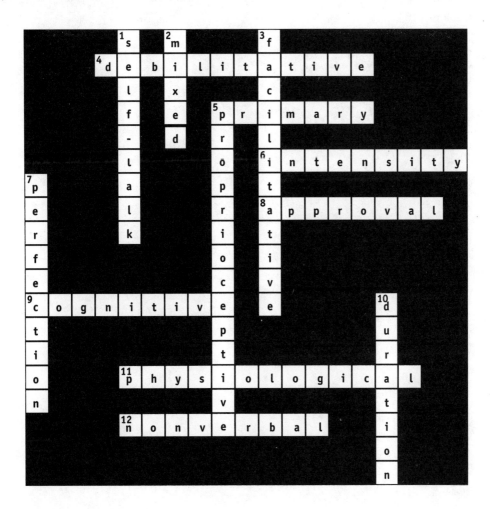

TRUE/FALSE

1. T		**3.** F		**5.** F		**7.** T		**9.** F
2. T		**4.** F		**6.** F		**8.** T		**10.** T

Harcourt Brace & Company

COMPLETION

1. catastrophic expectations
2. helplessness
3. causation
4. overgeneralization
5. shoulds
6. approval
7. perfection
8. activating event
9. monitoring
10. disputing

MULTIPLE CHOICE

1. a
2. f
3. c
4. b
5. g
6. d
7. d
8. c
9. g
10. a
11. e
12. e
13. f
14. b
15. b
16. c
17. d
18. c
19. a
20. d

Chapter 5

Language: Barrier and Bridge

OUTLINE

Use this outline to take notes as you read the chapter in the text and/or as your instructor lectures in class.

I. The nature of language

A. **Language Is Symbolic**

B. **Language Is Subjective**

C. **Language Is Rule-Governed**
   1. Phonological rules
   2. Syntactic rules
   3. Semantic rules
   4. Pragmatic rules - CMM theory

II. The impact of language

A. **Naming and Identity**

B. **Affiliation, Attraction, and Interest**
   1. Convergence
   2. Divergence
   3. Liking/interest
      a. Demonstrative pronoun choice
      b. Sequential placement
      c. Negation
      d. Duration

C. **Power**

III. Uses (and abuses) of language

A. **Precision and Vagueness**
   1. Equivocation
   2. Abstraction
      a. High abstraction advantages
         1) Shorthand
         2) Avoid confrontation
         3) Avoid embarrassment

            b. High abstraction problems
                1) Stereotyping
                2) Confuse others
                3) Confuse yourself
                4) Lack of relational clarity
            c. Specific behavioral language
                1) The participants
                2) The circumstances
                3) The behaviors
        3. Euphemism
        4. Relative language
        5. Static evaluation

    B. **The Language of Responsibility**
        1. "It" statements
        2. "But" statements
        3. Questions
        4. "I" and "You" language
            a. "I" language
                1) Describes behavior
                2) Describes feelings
                3) Describes consequences
            b. Advantages of "I" language
                1) Defense reduction
                2) Honesty
                3) Completeness
            c. Problems with "I" language
                1) Anger interferes
                2) Other still gets defensive
                3) Can sound artificial
        5. "We" language
                1) Builds constructive climate
                2) Can sound presumptuous

    C. **Disruptive Language**
        1. Fact-opinion confusion
        2. Fact-inference confusion
        3. Emotive language

IV. Gender and Language

    A. **Content**
        1. Some common topics
        2. Sex talk restricted to same gender
        3. Many topics vary by gender

    B. **Reasons for Communicating**
        1. Women–establish and maintain relationships
            a. Support
            b. Questions
            c. Frequency

Harcourt Brace & Company

2. Men–accomplish tasks
   a. Control
   b. Competition
   c. Practical value

C. **Conversational Style**

D. **Nongender Variables**
   1. Social orientation
   2. Occupation
   3. Sex roles

V. Language and Culture

A. **Verbal Communication Styles**
   1. Low context/high context (level of directness)
   2. Elaborate/succinct
   3. Formal/informal

B. **Language and Worldview**
   1. Linguistic determinism
   2. Sapir-Whorf hypothesis
   3. Linguistic relativism

KEY TERMS

Use these key terms to review major concepts from your text. Write the definition for each key term in the space to the right

abstraction ladder _____

abstractions _____

behavioral description _____

"but" statement _____

CMM theory _____

convergence _____

directness _____

disclaimers _____

divergence _____

elaborate _____

Harcourt Brace & Company

emotive language _____

equivocal language _____

euphemisms _____

fact-inference confusion _____

fact-opinion confusion _____

formality _____

hedges _____

hesitations _____

high-context cultures _____

"I" language _____

informality _____

intensifiers _____

"it" statements _____

language of power _____

language of responsibility _____

linguistic determinism _____

linguistic relativism _____

low-context cultures _____

phonological rules _____

polite forms _____

powerless speech mannerisms _____

pragmatic rules _____

relative language _____

Sapir-Whorf hypothesis _____

semantic rules _____

Harcourt Brace & Company

sex roles _____

static evaluation _____

stereotyping _____

subscripting _____

succinct _____

syntactic rules _____

tag questions _____

"we" statements _____

"you" language _____

ACTIVITIES

5.1 LABEL THE LANGUAGE

❖ Activity Type: Skill Builder

PURPOSE

To help you recognize and change the imprecise language described in Chapter 5 of *Looking Out/Looking In.*

INSTRUCTIONS

1. In groups, label the language contained in each of the sentences below as relative language, emotive terms, or equivocal language.
2. Rewrite each sentence in more precise language.
3. Write your own examples of each variety of language in the space provided.
4. Compare your answers with those of the other groups.

Example

I'm trying to diet, so give me a **small piece of cake.**

Language *Relative language* _____
Revised statement *I'm trying to diet, so give me a piece of cake about half the size of yours.*

1. I want to talk about **our relationship.**

    Language _____

    Revised statement _____

    _____

2. They're real **party people**.

    Language _____

    Revised statement _____

    _____

3. Helen is a **troublemaker**.

Language _____

Revised statement_____

_____

4. Our candidate is trying to bring about a more **peaceful** world.

Language _____

Revised statement_____

_____

5. We've known each other for a **long time**.

Language _____

Revised statement_____

_____

6. Your essay should be **brief**.

Language _____

Revised statement_____

_____

7. She's a very **mature** child for her age.

Language _____

Revised statement_____

_____

8. Your contribution will help make government **more responsible to the people**.

Language _____

Revised statement_____

_____

9. You know **what's best**.

Language _____

Revised statement_____

_____

10. He's a real **pest**.

Language _____

Revised statement_____

_____

11. Stanley is an **ethical** person.

Language _____

Revised statement_____

_____

12. We need to make some **changes** around here.

Language _____

Revised statement_____

_____

13. I need **room to breathe**.

Language _____

Revised statement_____

_____

14. Let's get her **something really nice**.

Language _____

Revised statement_____

_____

15. He's **prejudiced**.

Language _____

Revised statement_____

_____

16. Please leave **a brief message**.

Language _____

Revised statement_____

_____

17. You've got **really poor attendance**.

Language _____

Revised statement_____

_____

18. She is **too uptight**.

Language _____

Revised statement_____

_____

Now write your own examples of each type of language and revise the statements to illustrate alternative language.

1. Equivocal language _____

_____

Revised _____

_____

2. Relative language _____

_____

Revised _____

_____

5. Emotive language _____

_____

Revised _____

_____

Harcourt Brace & Company

5.2 BEHAVIORAL DESCRIPTIONS

❖ Activity Type: Skill Builder

PURPOSE

To increase the clarity of your language by using behavioral descriptions.

INSTRUCTIONS

In each of the situations below, describe the behavior of an individual that might have led to the statement about him or her.

Examples

John's full of action.
John rode his bike for an hour and then mowed the lawn.

Meg is so much fun to be with.
Meg went shopping in the mall with me and laughed with me about how we looked in the new, looser styles.

1. That teacher is a bore!

   _____

   _____

2. That guy's real macho.

   _____

   _____

3. She's an all-around good person.

   _____

   _____

4. Mike's a hard worker.

   _____

   _____

Harcourt Brace & Company

5. Mark's real laid-back.

_____

_____

6. Jill's such a dresser.

_____

_____

7. Josh is a real sport.

_____

_____

8. She gives me moral support.

_____

_____

9. Jack's motivated.

_____

_____

10. Peg is inspiring.

_____

_____

11. My parents are understanding.

_____

_____

12. Shelley's a flake!

_____

_____

13. You're too emotional.

_____

_____

14. He's so thoughtful.

_____

_____

5.3 LANGUAGE CLARITY

❖ Activity Type: Skill Builder

PURPOSE

To increase the clarity of your language by revising phrases to describe an idea or act.

INSTRUCTIONS

For each of the statements below, write a clear description of the idea or act to clarify to your partner your intentions. Record examples of your own at the end of the exercise.

Example

"Go over that way."
"Go across the footbridge, turn right, and go to the third building on your left."

1. Clean up your act.

_____

_____

2. This time, clean the car correctly.

_____

_____

3. Look more confident.

_____

_____

4. You add a bit of this and that and the sauce is finished.

_____

_____

5. This paper should be creative.

_____

_____

6. Make that report clearer.

_____

_____

7. Work harder on your studies.

_____

_____

8. Pay more attention.

_____

_____

9. Don't be so obnoxious!

_____

_____

10. Don't say things like that.

_____

_____

11. Clean up your room.

_____

_____

12. Be kind to your sister.

_____

_____

13. Get something good at the video store.

_____

_____

14. Fix a healthy dinner.

_____

_____

15. Show me that you care.

_____

_____

16. Your language is too pushy around my family.

_____

_____

17. You'll never get anywhere in the company talking like that.

_____

_____

18. You talk like a girl.

_____

_____

Now record unclear directions of your own and rewrite them with clear descriptions.

19. _____.

_____

_____

20. _____.

_____

_____

Harcourt Brace & Company

5.4 PRACTICING "I" LANGUAGE

◆❖ Activity Type: Skill Builder

PURPOSE

To give you practice speaking descriptively, instead of evaluatively.

INSTRUCTIONS

1. Rewrite each of the evaluative "you" language statements below using descriptive "I" language.

   Be careful to
   a. Use specific, low-level abstractions
   b. Take responsibility for your own thoughts and feelings (don't say , "I feel you are . . .")
   c. Avoided loaded terms like "you wouldn't <u>even</u>", "you could <u>at least</u>," finally, whenever, ever since, etc.

2. Record examples of your own at the end and rewrite them.

Example 1

"You don't care about my feelings."
"I felt hurt when I saw you in the restaurant with your old girlfriend when you told me you had to work."

EXAMPLE 2

"That was a dumb move!"
"Ever since you used the high setting to dry my favorite cotton shirt, it doesn't fit me anymore. That's why I'm so mad."

1. "You never want to hear my side of the story."

   _____

   _____

   _____

2. "You don't keep your word."

   _____

   _____

   _____

3. "You're no fun."

_____

_____

_____

4. "You can't take a joke."

_____

_____

_____

5. "Do you ever tell the truth?"

_____

_____

_____

6. "You exaggerate things."

_____

_____

_____

7. "You're making me crazy!"

_____

_____

_____

8. "You have a bad attitude."

_____

_____

_____

9. "You aren't there for me."

_____

_____

_____

10. "You ruined my day."

_____

_____

_____

11. "You're always in a bad mood."

_____

_____

_____

12. "You can never do anything because you always work"

_____

_____

_____

Record your own "you" language statements here. Rewrite them using "I" language.

13. _____.

_____

_____

14. _____.

_____

_____

15. _____.

_____

_____

5.5 "I" LANGUAGE

❖ Activity Type: Oral Skill

PURPOSE

To evaluate your skill in delivering "I" language statements.

INSTRUCTIONS

1. Form partners and identify situations in your lives in which both "you" and "I" language messages might be delivered.
2. Deliver in a realistic manner both a "you" message and an "I" message to your partner according to Chapter 5 of *Looking Out/Looking In* and outlined in the checklist below.
3. Describe on a separate sheet of paper

   a. how well "I" language might (or might not) work in the situation you have chosen. If you do not think "I" language is the best approach for this situation, explain why and describe a more promising alternative.

   b. the degree to which you could (or could not) increase your communicative competence by using "I" language in other situations.

CHECKLIST

_____   Delivers a "you" message to partner.

_____   Delivers the same message in "I" language, without using notes

        _____   Describes the other's specific behavior(s) in specific, behavior terms, using non-evluative language

        _____   Describes own feelings arising from other's behavior(s).

        _____   Describes consequences of other's behavior(s) as appropriate for self, for the other person, for third parties, or for the relationship.

_____   Verbal and nonverbal behavior

        _____   Reflects responsibility for "owning" the message.

        _____   Sounds realistic and consistent with personal style.

        _____   Evaluates probable outcome of "I" message, explaining how it might be used or adapted in this and other real-life situations.

5.6 EXAMINING YOUR LANGUAGE

◆ Activity Type: Invitation to Insight

PURPOSE

To help you analyze the types of language you use and the effectiveness of each.

INSTRUCTIONS

1. For each of the situations below, record the type of language used by the speaker. Evaluate its effectiveness. If you cannot identify with the situation, substitute one of your own.
2. Record the language you would use in response. Again, record your own situation and language if you have a relevant one.
3. Label the type of your language and its effectiveness. Focus on high and low abstraction, powerful or powerless speech mannerisms, facts or opinions, inferences, high- and low-context language styles and language and worldview.
4. Describe any alternative language you could use and its relative effectiveness.

Example

Situation: Your supervisor at work has called you aside three times this week to correct work you have done. Each time she says, "You've messed up on this."

Type of language used with you/effectiveness: *My supervisor used "you" language and high abstraction. It wasn't very effective with me because I wasn't sure exactly what I'd messed up on, and I got very defensive, thinking she was about to fire me. She was very direct with me, however; she didn't keep silent about what was bothering her (this is consistent with the low-context culture in which I live).*

Language you'd use: *"You're on me all the time about something or other."*

Type of language and effectiveness: *"You" language and high abstraction. This is probably not very effective. My supervisor is likely to get defensive. Actually, my supervisor may think this is "helpful" and "caring" behavior and not realize that I am feeling hassled and threatened.*

Alternative language: *"Ms. Gomez, I'm worried that I'm not doing my job correctly because you've corrected me three times this week." This "I" language is more likely to let Ms. Gomez know what specifically is bothering me without raising a good deal of defensiveness. She's likely to appreciate my directness and specific request for help.*

1. Situation: You borrowed your friend's car and returned it with about 1 gallon of gas in it because you were too rushed to fill it. Now she says to you: "I'm perhaps just a little bit upset with you. That was rotten, don't you think?"

Type of language used with you/effectiveness:

_____

_____

Language you'd use:

_____

_____

Type of language and effectiveness:

_____

_____

Alternative language:

_____

_____

2. Situation: You have a hard time saying "no." Lately your roommate has been asking you to do chores that are not your responsibility. Tonight the roommate says, "You're such a great roommate. You won't mind doing the dishes for me tonight since I've got a date and you're just staying home anyway, will you?"

Type of language used with you/effectiveness:

_____

_____

Language you'd use:

_____

_____

Type of language and effectiveness:

_____

_____

Harcourt Brace & Company

Alternative language:

_____

_____

3. Situation: Cousins of yours are moving to town. They just called, addressing you by your old family nickname and said, "You lucky person, you get to have the pleasure of our company for a while until we find a place to live."

Type of language used with you/effectiveness:

_____

_____

Language you'd use:

_____

_____

Type of language and effectiveness:

_____

_____

Alternative language:

_____

_____

4. Situation: You're working on a project with a partner from class, and the partner says, "We'll never get this done. You're too meticulous about everything."

Type of language used with you/effectiveness:

_____

_____

Language you'd use:

_____

_____

Harcourt Brace & Company

Type of language and effectiveness:

_____

_____

Alternative language:

_____

_____

5. Situation: Your boss's five-year-old is visiting the workplace. The child has broken two items and is now running from door to door, laughing loudly. Two customers look your way. Your boss says, "Chip off the old block, huh? Really an energetic kid!"

Type of language used with you/effectiveness:

_____

_____

Language you'd use:

_____

_____

Type of language and effectiveness:

_____

_____

Alternative language:

_____

_____

Record a situation of your own here:

6. Situation:

Type of language used with you/effectiveness:

_____

_____

Language you'd use:

_____

_____

Type of language and effectiveness:

_____

_____

Alternative language:

_____

_____

CROSSWORD PUZZLE

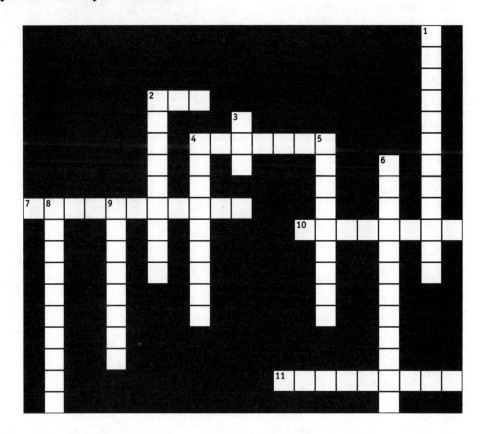

Across

2 a role that is the social orientation that governs language behavior, rather than the biological gender

4 language that conveys the sender's attitude rather than simply offering an objective description

7 a range of more to less specificity describing an event or object

10 rules of language that govern what meaning language has, as opposed to what structure it has

11 rules of language that govern what interpretation of a message is appropriate in a given context

Down

1 categorizing individuals according to a set of characteristics assumed to belong to all members of a group

2 rules of language that govern the ways symbols can be arranged, as opposed to the meanings of those symbols

3 language statement that expresses or implies a judgment of the other person

4 language that consists of words that have more than one commonly accepted definition

5 a pleasant term substituted for a blunt one in order to soften the impact of unpleasant information

6 rules of language that govern how sounds are combined to form words

8 descriptions that refer only to observable phenomena

9 language terms that gain their meaning by comparison

TRUE/FALSE

Mark the statements below as true or false. For statements that are false, correct them on the lines below to create a true statement.

_____ **1.** Words are not arbitrary symbols; they have meaning in and of themselves.

_____

_____ **2.** According to research, your name is likely to affect people's first impressions of you.

_____

_____ **3.** Since research shows that people are rated as more competent when their talk is free of powerless speech mannerisms, it is obvious that a consistently powerful style of speaking is always the best approach.

_____

_____ **4.** Ambiguity and vagueness are forms of language that are to be avoided at all costs.

_____

_____ **5.** Ohio's Antioch College's sexual conduct code uses low-level abstractions to minimize the chances of anyone claiming confusion about a partner's willingness to engage in sexual behavior.

_____

_____ **6.** "How are we feeling today?" is an example of "we" language.

_____

_____ **7.** "Democrats are more responsive to the people than Republicans are" is an example of a fact statement.

_____

_____ **8.** According to research on language and gender, on the average, men discuss with men different topics than women discuss with other women.

_____

_____ **9.** Men are more likely to use language to accomplish the job at hand, while women are are more likely to use language to nourish relationships.

_____

_____ **10.** A person from the United States is more likely to value direct language than is someone from Japan.

_____

COMPLETION

Fill in the blanks below with the correct terms chosen from the list below.

succinctness   equivocation   convergence   divergence   polite forms
tag questions   elaborateness   hedges disclaimers   subscripting

1. _____ is the process of adapting one's speech style to match that of others with whom the communicator wants to identify.

2. _____ in language use involve denying direct responsibility for the statement, such as "I could be wrong, but . . . "

3. _____ of language involve using respectful terms of address, such as "You're welcome, ma'am."

4. _____ involves speaking in a way that emphasizes a person's differences from the other persons with whom he or she is speaking .

5. _____ in language use involves using words that have more than one commonly accepted definition, such as "They eat _healthy_ food."

6. _____ in language use involve a negation statement, such as "_Didn't you think_ that party was boring?"

7. _____ in language use make less of the feeling or intention statement, such as "I'm _rather_ upset."

8. _____ in language use involves dating to reduce static evaluation, such as "Kanako$_{July\ 13}$ is nervous."

9. _____ involves speaking with few words, and it is usually most extreme in cultures where silence is valued.

10. _____ involves speaking with rich and expressive terms, sometimes involving strong assertions and exaggerations.

MULTIPLE CHOICE

Label the examples of language given below by writing the letter of the language type illustrated on the line in front of the example.

a. inference
b. relative word
c. euphemism
d. emotive word
e. equivocal language

_____ **1.** John didn't call **so he must be angry**.

_____ **2.** I have a **stomach problem**.

_____ **3.** That place is **expensive**.

_____ **4.** That guy is a real **hunk**.

_____ **5.** I'd like **recognition** for my work.

_____ **6.** The bathroom **needs some air**.

_____ **7.** We need to make **progress** tonight.

_____ **8.** The funeral director pointed out the **slumber room**.

_____ **9.** He showed up, **so he must agree**.

_____ **10.** That's a real **smart trick you pulled**.

_____ **11.** My brother is a **sanitation engineer**.

_____ **12.** Ian gave a **long** speech.

_____ **13.** My grandfather is **young**.

_____ **14.** My sister is a **pill**.

Choose the letter of the *least* abstract alternative to the high abstraction terms.

_____ **15.** Jo's **constantly complaining**.

    a. Jo whines a lot.
    b. Jo complains often about the workload.
    c. Jo told me three times this week that she feels overworked.
    d. Every time we meet, Jo complains about all the work she does.

_____ **16.** He can **never** do **anything** because he's **always busy**.

  a. He couldn't take me to the dinner because he had to work.
  b. He can never do anything fun because he's always working.
  c. He didn't ever take time off to be with me.
  d. He works too much so we have a boring life.

_____ **17.** There are **a lot of problems** associated with **freedom.**

  a. Freedom carries with it responsibility.
  b. Since I moved into my own apartment, I have to pay ten bills.
  c. I don't like all the responsibility of living on my own.
  d. My economic responsibilities limit my freedom.

_____ **18.** Shannon is **worthless** as a roommate.

  a. Shannon is always gone, so she's really not part of our house.
  b. Shannon never does her part around here.
  c. Shannon's jobs seldom get done around here.
  d. Shannon has attended only one of our six house meetings.

_____ **19.** Carlos is the **most wonderful friend**.

  a. Carlos has never told anyone about my fear of failing.
  b. Carlos listens to me about everything.
  c. Carlos is the best listener I've ever met.
  d. I can trust Carlos implicitly with all my secrets.

_____ **20.** Keiko **goes overboard** in trying to make people like her.

  a. Keiko gave everyone on the team a valentine.
  b.. Keiko is the biggest kiss-up you ever met.
  c. I think Keiko is trying to make my friends like her better than me.
  d. I want Keiko to stop trying to outdo everybody else.

CROSSWORD PUZZLE

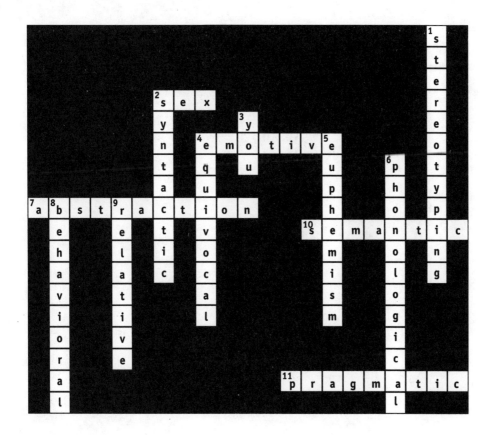

TRUE/FALSE

1. F	**3.** F	**5.** T	**7.** F	**9.** T
2. T	**4.** F	**6.** F	**8.** T	**10.** T

COMPLETION

1. convergence
2. disclaimers
3. polite forms
4. divergence
5. equivocation
6. tag questions
7. hedges
8. subscripting
9. succinctness
10. elaborateness

MULTIPLE CHOICE

1. a
2. c
3. b
4. d
5. e
6. c
7. e
8. c
9. a
10. d
11. c
12. b
13. b
14. d
15. c
16. a
17. b
18. d
19. a
20. a

Harcourt Brace & Company

Chapter 6

Nonverbal Communication: Messages without Words

OUTLINE

Use this outline to take notes as you read the chapter in the text and/or as your instructor lectures in class.

I. Nonverbal communication

A. Importance
1. Emotional impact
2. Greater percentage of social meaning

B. Definition: Those Messages Expressed by Other Than Linguistic Means

II. Characteristics of nonverbal communication

A. Nonverbal Communication Exists

B. Nonverbal Behavior Has Communicative Value
1. Deliberate
2. Unintentional

C. Nonverbal Communication Is Culture-Bound

D. Nonverbal Communication Is Primarily Relational
1. Identity management
2. Definition of relationships we want with others
3. Conveyance of emotion

E. Nonverbal Communication Serves Many Functions
1. Repeating
2. Substituting
3. Complementing
4. Accenting
5. Regulating
6. Contradicting

F. Nonverbal Communication Is Ambiguous

III. Differences between verbal and nonverbal communication

A. **Single versus Multiple Channels**

B. **Discrete versus Continuous**

C. **Clear versus Ambiguous**

D. **Verbal versus Nonverbal Impact**

E. **Deliberate versus Unconscious**

IV. Types of nonverbal communication

A. **Body Orientation**

B. **Posture**
1. Forward/backward lean
2. Tension/relaxation

C. **Gestures**
1. Preening behaviors
2. Manipulators

D. **Face and Eyes**
1. Complexity
2. Speed
3. Emotions reflected
4. Microexpression
5. Kinds of messages
   a. Involvement
   b. Positive/negative attitude
   c. Dominance/submission
   d. Interest (pupils)

E. **Voice (Paralanguage): Tone, Speed, Pitch, Number and Length of Pauses, Volume, Disfluencies**

F. **Touch**

G. **Physical Attractiveness**

H. **Clothing**

I. **Proxemics (Space)**
1. Intimate
2. Personal
3. Social
4. Public

J. **Territoriality**

K. **Physical Environment**

L. **Time (Chronemics)**

Harcourt Brace & Company

KEY TERMS

Use these key terms to review major concepts from your text. Write the definition for each key term in the space to the right.

accenting _____

affect blends _____

body orientation _____

chronemics _____

complementing _____

contradicting _____

deception cues _____

disfluencies _____

double messages _____

emblems _____

gestures _____

illustrators _____

intimate distance _____

kinesics _____

leakage _____

manipulators _____

microexpression _____

nonverbal communication _____

paralanguage _____

personal distance _____

posture _____

proxemics _____

public distance _____

regulating _____

repeating _____

social distance _____

substituting _____

tension cue _____

territory _____

ACTIVITIES

6.1 DESCRIBING NONVERBAL STATES

❖ Activity Type: Skill Builder

PURPOSE

To describe the nonverbal behaviors that indicate various emotional and attitudinal states.

INSTRUCTIONS

NOTE: Group members (or individuals) may want to make videotaped examples of their own behavior reflecting each of the situations below or they may want to collect television or movie examples illustrating the emotions and attitudes described below.

1. For each of the statements below, record the nonverbal behaviors that reflect the attitude or emotions described.
2. Compare your responses with those of others in the class and note the similarities and differences in your responses.

STATEMENT	NONVERBAL BEHAVIOR
Example She listens well.	Turns body toward me, leans forward, smiles once or twice, nods, maintains eye contact about 80 percent of the time.
1. He acts so cool.	
2. She's a tease.	
3. He's paranoid.	
4. She's flirting. (Use Table 6.2 from the text if you need help here.)	

Harcourt Brace & Company

STATEMENT	NONVERBAL BEHAVIOR
5. He's stressing out.	
6. She takes over.	
7. He's overdramatic.	
8. She acts confidently.	
9. He seems friendly.	
10. She's "hyper."	

COMPARISONS

Record the similarities and differences you found when comparing your responses to those of your classmates.

_____

_____

_____

_____

6.2 NONVERBAL COMPLAINTS

❖ Activity Type: Skill Builder

PURPOSE

To facilitate the display of nonverbally congruent behaviors.

INSTRUCTIONS

For each statement below, describe the nonverbal behaviors that might satisfy the person making the complaints. Compare your advice with that of others in the class, noting the differences different people or contexts may have on the advice.

COMPLAINT	NONVERBAL ADVICE
Example He says I'm too eager to please.	Take a little more time to respond after a request. Lean toward the person a little less. Smile, but don't keep the smile on your face continuously. Gesture, but don't gesture as quickly. Stand a little more erect and hold all the parts of your body more still.
1. She says I'm too serious.	
2. My boss says not to be so aggressive.	
3. He says I could be more helpful.	
4. Friend or relative says I don't really care about him or her.	
5. I sound stupid when I hear myself on tape.	
6. They look so sure of themselves, but I just can't act that way.	

Harcourt Brace & Company

COMPLAINT	NONVERBAL ADVICE
7. I'd like to look more relaxed.	
8. I don't want them to think I'm indifferent.	
9. She says I act too cold.	
10. He says I should be more open.	

Compare your advice with that of others in the class. Note any similarities or differences.

_____

_____

_____

_____

How might the persons involved or the context change the advice you would give?

_____

_____

_____

_____

_____

_____

6.3 NONVERBAL HOW-TO'S

❖ Activity Type: Skill Builder

PURPOSE

To define what you and others in the class consider effective nonverbal behavior in some social situations.

INSTRUCTIONS

1. For each of the social situations below, list the nonverbal behaviors you believe will achieve the stated goal.
2. Compare your answers with those of others in your class.
3. Reflect on the behavior of yourself and others important to you. How might you change some of the nonverbal cues you display to communicate what you desire more effectively?

SOCIAL SITUATIONS	NONVERBAL BEHAVIOR
Example Initiate conversation with a stranger at a party.	Make eye contact, offer hand in greeting, smile, come within four feet of other person, turn body toward other person, nod occasionally when other is talking.
1. Take control or exercise leadership in a class group.	
2. Come across well in a job interview.	
3. Tell an interesting joke or story.	
4. Appear friendly and warm.	
5. Signal your desire to leave a conversation when the other person keeps on talking.	
6. Appear confident when asking boss for a raise.	

SOCIAL SITUATIONS	NONVERBAL BEHAVIOR
7. Appear interested in class lecture.	
8. Avoid talking with an undesirable person.	
9. Let a friend know you need to leave.	
10. Appear concerned about a friend's dilemma.	

Compare your answers with others in class. Note the areas of agreement and disagreement.

_____

_____

_____

_____

_____

_____

Are there situations or contexts in which the described behaviors could be changed to appear more effective?

_____

_____

_____

_____

_____

_____

If you could ask someone close to you to change his or her nonverbal behavior in a certain situation, what would you ask him or her to change and how would you tell him or her to communicate more effectively nonverbally?

_____

_____

_____

_____

_____

_____

6.4 EVALUATING AMBIGUITY

◆ Activity Type: Invitation to Insight

PURPOSE

1. To analyze the verbal and nonverbal aspects of your communication behaviors.
2. To weigh the consequences of sending congruent versus ambiguous messages.

INSTRUCTIONS

1. In each of the following situations, describe verbal and nonverbal behaviors likely to occur. Use descriptions of the twelve types of nonverbal communication described in Chapter 6 of *Looking Out/Looking In* (e.g., body orientation, posture, gesture, face and eyes, voice, touch, physical attractiveness, clothing, proxemics, territoriality, physical environment and time). Nonverbal behaviors seldom occur alone, so describe clusters of at least 3 nonverbal behaviors for each situation. Note whether the verbal and nonverbal behaviors are ambiguous or congruent (congruent means they send the same, consistent message). Finally, evaluate the possible consequences of the ambiguity or congruency.
2. Next describe four situations from your own life and how you would send verbal and nonverbal messages. Include a brief discussion of the consequences of your congruent or ambiguous behaviors.
3. After you've completed the examples, answer the questions about congruency/ambiguity here:

Consider situations in addition to the examples in this exercise when answering the following questions.

In what situations should you express yourself ambiguously? Explain how sending one message verbally and another one nonverbally could be beneficial.

_____

_____

_____

_____

Describe situations in which ambiguity is not desirable. Describe how you could best match your verbal and nonverbal behaviors in these situations.

_____

_____

_____

_____

Harcourt Brace & Company

SITUATION	YOUR VERBAL BEHAVIOR	YOUR NONVERBAL BEHAVIOR (USE A CLUSTER OF BEHAVIORS HERE)	ARE THE VERBAL/ NONVERBAL MESSAGES AMBIGUOUS?	POSSIBLE CONSEQUENCES
Example Person I like a lot takes me out to dinner and I have a good time and enjoy the food.	"I'm really enjoying this; the food is terrific and so is the company."	I look at my partner when I talk, smiling and tilting my head slightly forward. I lean toward my partner and touch my partner lightly on the arm and hand.	My verbal and nonverbal behaviors are not ambiguous in this context.	I hope the consequences are that my partner will understand how much I care and enjoy our time together. I run the risk of not "game playing," of course—in that I could be hurt if my partner's feelings don't match mine, but I think the chances are pretty slim in this instance.
1. My boss asks me to work late when I've made other plans.				
2. My roommate asks, while I'm doing homework, if I can make dinner.				

Harcourt Brace & Company

SITUATION	YOUR VERBAL BEHAVIOR	YOUR NONVERBAL BEHAVIOR (USE A CLUSTER OF BEHAVIORS HERE)	ARE THE VERBAL/ NONVERBAL MESSAGES AMBIGUOUS?	POSSIBLE CONSEQUENCES
3. My relative drops in to visit me when other people are over for the evening.				
4. My lab partner suggests that we go out partying together Friday night.				
5. Waiter grabs my plate and asks if I'm finished while food is still on my plate.				

SITUATION	YOUR VERBAL BEHAVIOR	YOUR NONVERBAL BEHAVIOR (USE A CLUSTER OF BEHAVIORS HERE)	ARE THE VERBAL/ NONVERBAL MESSAGES AMBIGUOUS?	POSSIBLE CONSEQUENCES
1.				
2.				
3.				
4.				
5.				

Harcourt Brace & Company

CROSSWORD PUZZLE

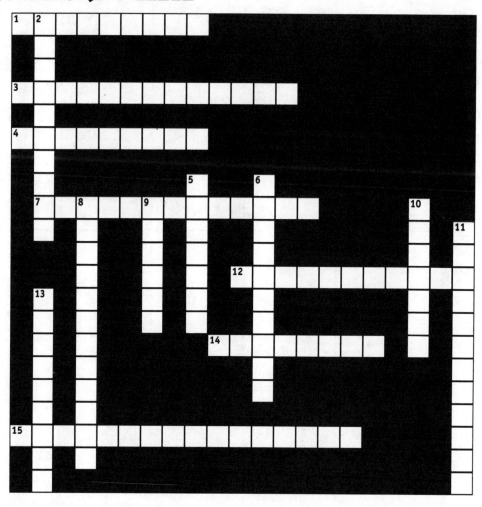

Across

1 nonverbal behavior that emphasizes part of a verbal message
3 nonverbal behavior that is inconsistent with a verbal message
4 nonverbal behavior cues that signal the untruthfulness of a verbal message
7 nonverbal behavior that reinforces a verbal message
12 nonverbal behavior that accompanies and supports verbal messages
14 the study of body position and motion
15 brief facial expressions

Down

2 the study of how humans use and structure time
5 nonverbal behaviors that reveal information a communicator does not disclose verbally
6 a nonlinguistic verbalization like um, er, ah
8 movements in which one part of the body grooms, massages, rubs, holds, fidgets, pinches, picks or otherwise manipulates another part
9 deliberate nonverbal behavior with precise meaning, known to virtually all members of a cultural group
10 the way in which individuals carry themselves: erect, slumping, and so on
11 nonlinguistic means of vocal expression: rate, pitch, tone, and so on
13 the study of how people and animals use space

Harcourt Brace & Company

TRUE/FALSE

Mark the statements below as true or false. Correct statements that are false on the lines below to create a true statement.

_____ **1.** Nonverbal behaviors are, by their nature, intentional.

_____

_____ **2.** Certain nonverbal behaviors like smiling are universal, and thus they are used and interpreted similarly around the world.

_____

_____ **3.** The concept of nonverbal convergence illustrates that skilled communicators can adapt their behavior when interacting with members of other cultures or subcultures in order to make the exchange more smooth and effective.

_____

_____ **4.** Nonverbal communication is much better suited to expressing attitudes and feelings than it is to expressing ideas.

_____

_____ **5.** Research on nonverbal communication and lying shows that individuals who are trying to deceive others are more likely to show nonverbal evidence of lying if they haven't had a chance to rehearse their lying and when they feel strongly about the information being hidden.

_____

_____ **6.** In studies of detecting lying, men are consistently more accurate than women at detecting the lies and discovering the underlying truth.

_____

_____ **7.** Both verbal and nonverbal messages are communicated one at a time, rather like pearls on a string.

_____

_____ **8.** Unlike verbal communication that is discrete (has a clear beginning and end), nonverbal communication is continuous and never ending.

_____

Harcourt Brace & Company

_____ **9.** The nonverbal impact of messages is more powerful than the verbal impact.

_____

_____ **10.** Nonverbal communication is clearer than verbal communication.

_____

COMPLETION

Fill in the blanks below with the correct terms chosen from the list below.

intimate	personal	social	public	relaxation
paralanguage	emblem	affect blend	touch	body orientation

1. _____ is the distance zone identified by Hall that ranges from four to about twelve feet; within it are the kinds of communication that usually occur in business.

2. _____ is a postural cue such as leaning back or lowering shoulders that a higher status person usually exhibits when not feeling threatened.

3. _____ is a deliberate, nonverbal behavior that has a very precise meaning known to virtually everyone within a cultural group.

4. _____ is the distance zone identified by Hall that ranges from eighteen inches to four feet and includes behavior found in most social conversations.

5. _____ is the combination of two or more expressions in different parts of the face.

6. _____ is the degree to which we face toward or away from someone with our body, feet, and head.

7. _____ is the distance zone identified by Hall that ranges from skin contact to about eighteen inches; we usually use this distance with people in private who are emotionally very close to us.

8. _____ is the distance zone identified by Hall that ranges from twelve feet outward and includes communication such as that found in a typical classroom.

9. _____ is nonverbal behavior that includes having a foreign accent.

10. _____ is nonverbal behavior that includes brushing up against someone.

Harcourt Brace & Company

MULTIPLE CHOICE

Choose the letter of the type of nonverbal communication that is illustrated below.

a. environment   b. paralinguistics   c. proxemics   d. territoriality

_____ **1.** No one dared to sit in Ralph's chair.

_____ **2.** Jeremy put a "NO ENTRANCE" sign on his door.

_____ **3.** The students rearranged the chairs in the classroom.

_____ **4.** Manuela stepped back three feet from her friend.

_____ **5.** The lovers were sitting only inches apart.

_____ **6.** Rob's voice softened when he spoke to her.

_____ **7.** There was a long pause after the decision was made.

_____ **8.** Mitchell sighed audibly.

_____ **9.** Gretchen took the third seat down from Yayoi.

_____ **10.** Kevin was annoyed that someone was leaning on his car.

a. body orientation   b. gesture   c. touch   d. face and eyes

_____ **11.** The children playfully kicked one another.

_____ **12.** Professor Jimenez illustrated her lecture with many arm movements.

_____ **13.** Leland shifted his shoulders toward the speaker.

_____ **14.** Ernie avoided looking at her.

_____ **15.** The executive stared at her employee.

_____ **16.** Martin turned his body away from his brother.

_____ **17.** The officer pointed in the correct direction.

_____ **18.** Letoya didn't appreciate the slap on the back.

_____ **19.** Blake set his jaw in disgust.

_____ **20.** Francesca signaled "OK" across the room.

CROSSWORD PUZZLE

Across / Down grid:

1. accenting
2. chronemics
3. contradicting
4. deception
7. complementing
12. illustrator
13. proxemics
14. kinesics
15. microexpressions

Down: manipulate, emblem, leakage, message, posture, paralanguage

TRUE/FALSE

1. F	3. T	5. T	7. F	9. T
2. T	4. T	6. F	8. T	10. F

COMPLETION

1. social
2. relaxation
3. emblem
4. personal

5. affect blend
6. body orientation
7. intimate
8. public

9. paralanguage
10. touch

MULTIPLE CHOICE

1. d
2. d
3. a
4. c

5. c
6. b
7. b
8. b

9. c
10. d
11. c
12. b

13. a
14. d
15. d
16. a

17. b
18. c
19. d
20. b

Harcourt Brace & Company

ACTIVITIES

7.1 LISTENING DIARY

◆ Activity Type: Invitation to Insight

PURPOSES

1. To help you identify the styles of listening you use in your interpersonal relationships.
2. To help you discover the consequences of the listening styles you use.

BACKGROUND

Looking Out/Looking In identifies several styles of effective and ineffective listening that you can use when seeking information from another:

pseudolistening	insensitive listening
stage hogging	ambushing
selective listening	prompting
insulated listening	questioning
defensive listening	paraphrasing

INSTRUCTIONS

1. Use the following form to record the listening styles you use in various situations.
2. After completing your diary, record your conclusions here.

Based on your observations, what styles of effective and ineffective listening do you use most often? In what situations do you use each of these styles? (Consider the people involved, the time, subject, and your personal mood when determining situational variables.)

_____

_____

_____

_____

What are the consequences of using the listening styles you have just described?

_____

_____

_____

_____

TIME AND PLACE	PEOPLE	SUBJECT	LISTENING STYLE(S)	CONSEQUENCES
Example Saturday night party	my date and several new acquaintances	good backpacking trips	*stage hogging*: I used everybody's remarks to show what a hotshot explorer I am.	I guess I was trying to get everyone to like me. My egotistical attitude probably accomplished the opposite!
1.				
2.				
3.				

7.2 RESPONSES TO PROBLEMS

❖ Activity Type: Skill Builder

PURPOSE

To help you practice the various styles of responding to others' problems.

INSTRUCTIONS

For each of the problem statements below, write a response in each style of helping discussed in *Looking Out/Looking In.* Make your response as realistic as possible. Then record a situation of your own and write listening responses for it.

Example

"I don't know what to do. I tried to explain to my professor why the assignment was late, but he wouldn't even listen to me."

Advising *You ought to write him a note. He might be more open if he has time to read it and think about it.*

Judging *You have to accept these things. Moping won't do any good, so quit feeling sorry for yourself.*

Analyzing *I think the reason he wasn't sympathetic is because he hears lots of excuses this time of year.*

Supporting *All of your work has been so good that I'm sure this one assignment won't matter. Don't worry!*

Questioning *What did he say? Do you think he'll change his mind later? How could you make up the assignment?*

Prompting *(Short silence) And so . . . ?*

Paraphrasing *You sound really discouraged, since he didn't even seem to care about your reasons–is that it?*

1. My girlfriend says she wants to date other guys this summer while I'm out in the boondocks working on construction. She claims it's just to keep busy and that it won't make any difference with us, but I think she wants to break off permanently, and she's trying to do it gently.

   Advising _____

   _____

   Judging _____

   _____

Harcourt Brace & Company

Analyzing _____

_____

Supporting _____

_____

Questioning _____

_____

Prompting_____

_____

Paraphrasing _____

_____

2. My roommate and I can't seem to get along. She's always having her boyfriend over, and he doesn't know when to go home. I don't want to move out, but I can't put up with this much longer. If I bring it up I know my roommate will get defensive, though.

Advising _____

_____

Judging _____

_____

Analyzing _____

_____

Supporting _____

_____

Questioning _____

_____

Prompting_____

_____

Paraphrasing _____

_____

5. What do you do about a friend who borrows things and doesn't return them?

Advising _____

_____

Judging _____

_____

Analyzing _____

_____

Supporting _____

_____

Questioning _____

_____

Prompting_____

_____

Paraphrasing _____

_____

4. The pressure of going to school and doing all the other things in my life is really getting to me. I can't go on like this, but I don't know where I can cut back.

Advising _____

_____

Judging _____

_____

Analyzing _____

_____

Supporting _____

_____

Questioning _____

_____

Prompting_____

_____

Paraphrasing _____

_____

5. You think that by the time you become an adult your parents would stop treating you like a child, but not mine! If I wanted their advice about how to live my life, I'd ask.

Advising _____

_____

Judging _____

_____

Analyzing _____

_____

Supporting _____

_____

Questioning _____

_____

Prompting_____

_____

Paraphrasing _____

_____

6. (record a situation of your own here) _____

_____

Advising _____

_____

Judging _____

_____

Analyzing _____

_____

Supporting _____

_____

Questioning _____

_____

Prompting_____

_____

Paraphrasing _____

_____

Harcourt Brace & Company

7.3 PARAPHRASING PRACTICE

❖ Activity Type: Skill Builder

PURPOSE

To develop your ability to paraphrase in order to gain information about another person's thoughts.

INSTRUCTIONS

Write a paraphrasing response for each of the following statements. Include the speaker's thoughts and, as appropriate, the speaker's feelings. Remember to do at least one of the following to avoid repeating:

1. Change the wording
2. Offer an example
3. Look for the underlying theme

Example

"It's not fair that I have to work so much. Other students can get better grades because they have the time to study."
So your job is taking time away from your studies and you think you're at a
disadvantage?

1. "I guess it's OK for you to use my computer. Just be careful to handle the disks carefully, and don't put any food or drinks on the desk or anywhere near the machine. This computer cost me a lot of money, and it would be a disaster if anything happened to it."

   _____

   _____

   _____

2. "You'll have the best chance at getting a loan for the new car you want if you give us a complete financial statement and credit history."

   _____

   _____

   _____

3. (Instructor to student) "This paper shows a lot of promise. It could probably earn you an A grade if you just develop the idea about the problems that arise from poor listening a bit more."

_____

_____

_____

4. "I do like the communication course, but it's not at all what I expected. It's much more *personal*, if you know what I mean."

_____

_____

_____

5. "We just got started on your car's transmission. I'm pretty sure we can have it ready tonight."

_____

_____

_____

6. "I do think it's wrong to take any lives, but sometimes I think certain criminals deserve capital punishment."

_____

_____

_____

7. "We are planning to have some friends over tonight, but I guess you're welcome to come too. Why don't you just bring along something we can munch on so we'll be sure to have enough food?"

_____

_____

_____

Harcourt Brace & Company

8. "You know I enjoy spending time with you. But I have other friends, too!"

_____

_____

_____

7.4 LISTENING FOR FEELINGS

❖ Activity Type: Skill Builder

PURPOSE

To help you identify the feelings that are often implied but not stated by others.

INSTRUCTIONS

For each of the statements below, write the feeling or feelings that the speaker might be experiencing.

POSSIBLE FEELINGS	SPEAKER'S REMARKS
Example puzzlement, hurt	It seems like you haven't been paying much attention to me lately. Is there something wrong?
1.	I wonder if I ought to start looking for another job. They're reorganizing the company, and what with a drop in business and all, maybe this is one of the jobs they'll cut back on. But if my boss finds out I'm looking around, maybe he'll think I don't like it here and let me go anyway.
2.	It was a great game. I played a lot, I guess, but I only scored once. The coach put Ryan in ahead of me.
3.	I said I'd do the collecting for him, but I sure don't feel like it. But I owe him a favor, so I guess I'll have to do it.
4.	I've got a report due tomorrow, an exam the next day, rehearsals every night this week, and now a meeting this afternoon. I don't think I can even fit in eating, and this has been going on all month.
5.	Sure she gets better grades than I do. She's a housewife, takes only two classes, and all she has to do is study. I have to work a job and go to school, too. And I don't have anyone to support me.

POSSIBLE FEELINGS	SPEAKER'S REMARKS
6.	I can't understand why they haven't written. They've never been gone this long without at least a card, and I don't even know how to get in touch with them.
7.	We had a great evening last night. The dinner was fantastic; so was the party. We saw lots of people; Erin loves that sort of thing.
8.	My daughter got straight A's this year, and the high school has a reputation for being very hard. She's a natural student. But sometimes I wonder if she isn't all books. I wish I could help her get interested in something besides studying.
9.	Boy, the teacher tells us he'll mark off on our grade every time we're late, but it doesn't seem to bother him when he comes in late. He must figure it's his privilege.
10.	I worked up that whole study–did all the surveying, the compiling, the writing. It was my idea in the first place. But he turned it in to the head office with his name on it, and he got the credit.
11.	I don't know whether I'm doing a good job or not. She never tells me if I'm doing well or need to work harder. I sure hope she likes my work.
12.	She believed everything he said about me. She wouldn't even listen to my side, just started yelling at me.
13.	Look, we've gone over and over this. The meeting could have been over an hour ago if we hadn't gotten hung up on this one point. If we can't make a decision, let's table it and move on.
14.	Look, I know I acted like a rat. I apologized, and I'm trying to make up for it. I can't do anymore, can I? So drop it!
15.	How can I tell him how I really feel? He might get mad and then we'd start arguing. He'll think I don't love him if I tell him my real feelings.

Harcourt Brace & Company

7.5 PROBLEM-SOLVING PARAPHRASING

◆❖ Activity Type: Skill Builder

PURPOSE

To help you become skillful at giving paraphrasing responses to others' problems.

BACKGROUND

You have already learned that the most helpful paraphrasing responses reflect both the speaker's thoughts and feelings. In order for this style of helping to be effective, you also have to sound like yourself, and not another person or a robot. There are many ways to reflect another's thoughts and feelings:

> "It sounds like you're . . ."
> "I hear you saying . . ."
> "Let me see if I've got it. You're saying . . ."
> "So you're telling me . . ."

INSTRUCTIONS

Write a paraphrasing response for each of the statements that follow. Be sure that the response fits your style of speaking, while at the same time it reflects the speaker's *thoughts* and *feelings*.

Example

"Stan always wants to tell me about the women he's going out with; he gives me 'blow-by-blow' descriptions of their dates that take hours, and he never seems to ask about who I'm going out with or what I'm interested in."
"It seems like you might be tired (feeling) of hearing about Stan's love life (thoughts) and maybe a little put-out (feeling) that he doesn't solicit information from you about whom you're dating (thoughts)—is that it?"

1. "I can't believe it! First the instructor said my answers were too skimpy, so I gave her more information. Now she tells me I'm being too wordy. Arggh!"

    _____

    _____

    _____

Harcourt Brace & Company

2. "What would you do if you heard your best friend making fun of you behind your back?"

_____

_____

_____

3. "We can't decide whether to put Grandmother in a nursing home. She hates the idea, but she can't take care of herself anymore, and it's just too much for us."

_____

_____

_____

4. "Those damn finals are finally over. I'm never going to even _think_ about history again!"

_____

_____

_____

5. "I'm really starting to hate my job. Every day I do the same boring, mindless work. But if I quit, I might not find any better work."

_____

_____

_____

6. "They haven't called me in ages. I think they must be mad at me or something."

_____

_____

_____

7. "Maybe I'll just use their lawn as a bathroom. Then they'll understand what their dog is doing to my yard!"

_____

_____

_____

8. "Why don't you try to be a little less messy around here? This place looks like a dump!"

_____

_____

_____

7.6 PARAPHRASING INFORMATION

❖ Activity Type: Skill Builder

INSTRUCTIONS

1. Join with three partners to create a foursome. Label the members A, B, C, and D.
2. A and B review the list below, choosing the topic upon which they disagree most widely.
3. A and B conduct a five-minute conversation on the topic they have chosen. During this period, the speakers may not express their own ideas until they have paraphrased the other person's position to his or her satisfaction. (If A and B finish discussing one item, they should move on to a second one from the list below.)
   C observes A   D observes B
4. At the end of the conversation, the observers should review the listening with the persons they observed.
5. Steps 1–5 are now repeated with the roles of conversationalists and observers reversed.

TOPICS

Indicate your position on each statement below by circling one of the following labels:

TA = totally agree   A = agree   D = disagree   TD = totally disagree

1. Despite the value of classes like this one, in the last analysis good communicators are born, not made.	**TA**	**A**	**D**	**TD**
2. One measure of a person's effectiveness as a communicator is how well he or she is liked by others.	**TA**	**A**	**D**	**TD**
3. No matter how unreasonable or rude they are, people deserve to be treated with respect.	**TA**	**A**	**D**	**TD**
4. An effective communicator should be able to handle any situation in a way that leaves the other person feeling positive about the interaction.	**TA**	**A**	**D**	**TD**
5. Interpersonal communication classes should be a required part of everyone's college education.	**TA**	**A**	**D**	**TD**
6. Most of what is taught in interpersonal communication classes is really common sense.	**TA**	**A**	**D**	**TD**

OR as an alternative

1. Choose a topic of interest to you and a partner (music, politics, religion, men, women, morals, etc.). It is best if you anticipate some difference of opinion on the topic.
2. Take turns stating your opinion. The only rule is that before you can take your turn stating *your* opinion, you must paraphrase the content of your partner's opinion *to his or her satisfaction.*

7.7 LISTENING AND RESPONDING STYLES

❖ Activity Type: Oral Skill

PURPOSE

To give you practice in using different listening styles to enhance listening effectiveness.

INSTRUCTIONS

1. With a partner, decide on communication situations that require effective listening. The situations should be real for the person describing them and might involve a problem, a decision that needs to be made, an issue of importance, or a change in a relationship.
2. Have your partner tell you the problem/issue/decision/relationship while you listen effectively.
3. You then tell your partner of your problem/issue/decision/relationship while your partner listens effectively.
4. Analyze the listening styles you used. Which were most/least effective in this situation? Which styles do you need to work on?
5. Use the checklist below to evaluate listening effectiveness.

CHECKLIST

5 = Superior   4 = Excellent   3 = Good   2 = Fair   1 = Poor

Uses appropriate language and nonverbal behaviors that   _____
  -demonstrate genuine interest
  -seem compatible with your personal communication style

Uses a balance of the following types of helping responses, as appropriate   _____

  <u>For both understanding and supporting</u>

  prompting

  genuine questions   _____

  paraphrasing   _____

    concisely and clearly reflects speaker's *thoughts*   _____

    concisely and clearly reflects speaker's *feelings*   _____

    requests confirmation of paraphrase accuracy   _____

  <u>For supporting only (as appropriate)</u>

  analyzing

  advising   _____

  supporting (comforting, praising, agreeing, humor)   _____

Based on self-observation (class feedback, videotape, etc.) and personal reflection

Which listening styles did you rely on most in this situation? _____

Which listening styles were most/least effective in this situation? _____

Which combination of responses could you have used in this situation, and which could you use in the future to be most effective? _____

Total _____

CROSSWORD PUZZLE

Across

1   a style of helping in which the receiver seeks additional information from the sender
3   a response in which the words of the speaker are repeated
5   a response style in which the receiver reassures, comforts, or distracts the person seeking help
9   using silences and brief statements of encouragement to draw out a speaker
12 a response style in which the receiver responds only to messages that interest him or her
13 the physiological dimensions of listening
14 an ineffective listening style in which the listener accepts the speaker's words at face value, resulting in failure to recognize the thoughts or feelings that are not directly expressed by the speaker
15 a response style in which the receiver perceives a speaker's comments as an attack

Down

2   occurs when sense is made of a message
4   an imitation of true listening in which the receiver's mind is elsewhere
6   giving observable feedback to the speaker
7   a reaction in which the receiver evaluates the sender's message either favorably or unfavorably
8   a helping response in which the receiver offers suggestions about how the speaker should deal with a problem
10 restating a speaker's thoughts and feelings in the listener's own words
11 an ineffective listening style in which the receiver ignores undesirable information

Harcourt Brace & Company

TRUE/FALSE

Mark the statements below as true or false. Correct statements that are false on the lines below to create a true statement.

_____ **1.** We spend more time listening to others than in any other type of communication.

_____

_____ **2.** Speaking is active; listening is passive.

_____

_____ **3.** All interruptions are attempts at stage hogging.

_____

_____ **4.** Given the onslaught of messages to listen to every day, it is understandable (and perhaps even justifiable) to use pseudolistening and other nonlistening responses.

_____

_____ **5.** In careful listening, the heart rate quickens and respiration increases.

_____

_____ **6.** People speak at about the same rate as others are capable of understanding their speech.

_____

_____ **7.** The advantages of listening are more obvious to people than the advantages of speaking.

_____

_____ **8.** Paraphrasing is the most accurate listening response you can make.

_____

_____ **9.** Judging listening responses may be favorable or negative.

_____

_____ **10.** Even an accurate form of analytic listening can create defensiveness since it may imply superiority and evaluativeness.

_____

COMPLETION

Fill in the blanks below with the correct terms chosen from the list below.

residual message   shift-response   conversational narcissist
sincere question   counterfeit question   constructive criticism
agreement   praise   reassurance
diversion

1. _____ is a name given to a nonlistening stage hog.

2. _____ is a genuine request for new information aimed at understanding others.

3. _____ is the information we store (remember) after processing information from teachers, friends, radio, TV, and other sources.

4. _____ is a type of state-hogging strategy in which the focus of the conversation is changed from the speaker to the stage hog.

5. _____ is a query that is a disguised attempt to send a message, not receive one.

6. _____ is a lesser form of negative judgment which is intended to help the problem-holder improve in the future.

7. _____ is a listening response that helps speakers by getting their minds off their troubles and on to something else.

8. _____ is a listening response that supports others by telling them how wonderful they are.

9. _____ is a listening response that encourages others to go on despite the problems of the immediate situation.

10. _____ is a listening response designed to show solidarity with speakers by telling them how right they are.

MULTIPLE CHOICE

Match the letter of the listening type with its example found below.

a. advising   c. analyzing   e. supporting   g. paraphrasing
b. judging   d. questioning   f. prompting

_____ 1. "So what do you mean?"

_____ 2. "You're mad at me for postponing the meeting?"

_____ 3. "You're probably just more upset than usual because of the stress of exams."

_____ 4. "What reason did she give for not attending?"

_____ 5. "Well, that was good of him not to complain."

_____ 6. "Have you tried praising her?"

_____ 7. "Have you tried talking to him about it?"

_____ 8. "Are you as excited as you sound about this big meet?"

_____ 9. "Jim should not have said that to Amy after you asked him not to."

_____ 10. "And then what happened?"

_____ 11. "So why did you go to Ellie's in the first place?"

_____ 12. "You really are good; they'll recognize that."

_____ 13. "It's not fair for you to have to work nights."

_____ 14. "Maybe you should give her a taste of her own medicine."

_____ 15. "And so you feel like retaliating because you're hurt?"

_____ 16. "Maybe you're a little insecure because of the divorce?"

_____ 17. "Like what?"

_____ 18. "What makes you think that he's cheating?"

_____ 19. "You've always pulled out those grades before—I know you can do it again."

_____ 20. "She's probably jealous so that's why she's doing that."

Choose the best informational paraphrasing response to each statement below.

21. Boss to employee: "Draft a letter that denies this request for a refund, but make it tactful."

    a. "What do you want me to say?"
    b. "How can I say no tactfully?"
    c. "So I should explain nicely why we can't give a refund, right?"
    d. "In other words, you want me to give this customer the brush-off?"

22. Friend says, "How do they expect us to satisfy the course requirements when there aren't enough spaces in the classes we're supposed to take?"

   a. "So you're frustrated because you can't get into the courses you need, huh?"
   b. "You think that some of the courses are worthless–is that it?"
   c. "Sounds like you're sorry you chose this major."
   d. "Why don't you write a letter to the chairperson of the department?"

23. Friend says, "Why don't I meet you after class at the student union?"

   a. "So you want me to pick you up at the student union?"
   b. "You want me to pick you up *again*?"
   c. "So we'll meet at the south entrance around 5:15?"
   d. "Why can't you drive yourself? Is your car broken again?"

24. Co-worker advises, "When you go in for a job interview, be sure and talk about the internship, your coursework, and your extracurricular activities. Don't expect them to ask you."

   a. "You think they won't ask about those things?"
   b. "Won't that sound like bragging?"
   c. "Why should I talk about the internship?"
   d. "So you're saying not to be bashful about stressing my experience?"

25. Friend says, "I don't think it's right that they go out and recruit women when there are plenty of good men around."

   a. "Sounds like you're angry because you think they're so concerned about being fair to women that they're being unfair to men, right?"
   b. "You're right–that doesn't sound fair."
   c. "If you don't think it's fair, you ought to speak up."
   d. "I can see that you're angry. What makes you think women are being given an unfair advantage?"

For each of the statements below, identify which response is the most complete and accurate problem-solving reflection of the speaker's thoughts and feelings.

26. "Sometimes I think I'd like to drop out of school, but then I start to feel like a quitter."

   a. "Maybe it would be helpful to take a break. You can always come back, you know."
   b. "You're afraid that you might fail if you stay in school now, is that it?"
   c. "I can really relate to what you're saying. I feel awkward here myself sometimes."
   d. "So you'd feel ashamed of yourself if you quit now, even though you'd like to?"

27. "I don't want to go to the party. I won't know anyone there, and I'll wind up sitting by myself all night."

    a. "You're afraid that you won't be able to approach anybody and nobody will want to talk to you?"
    b. "You never know; you could have a great time."
    c. "So you really don't want to go, eh?"
    d. "What makes you think it will be that way?"

28. "I get really nervous talking to my professor. I keep thinking that I sound stupid."

    a. "Talking to her is really a frightening experience?"
    b. "You're saying that you'd rather not approach her?"
    c. "You get the idea that she's evaluating you, and that leaves you feeling uncomfortable?"
    d. "You think that talking to her might affect your grade for the worse?"

29. "I don't know what to do about my kids. Their whining is driving me crazy."

    a. "Even though whining is natural, it's getting to you?"
    b. "Sometimes you really get fed up with their complaining?"
    c. "You're getting angry at them?"
    d. "Even the best parents get irritated sometimes."

30. "I just blew another test in that class. Why can't I do better?"

    a. "You probably need to study harder. You'll get it!"
    b. "You're feeling sorry for yourself because you've done all you can do and you still can't pull a better grade?"
    c. "Where do you think the problem is?"
    d. "You're discouraged and frustrated because you don't know what you're doing wrong?"

Harcourt Brace & Company

CROSSWORD PUZZLE

```
                    1q  2u  e   s   t   i   o   n   i   n   g
                        n
                        d
                    3v  e   r   b   a   t   i   m
            4p          r
            s       5s  u   p   p   o   6r  t   i   n   g                   7j
    8a      e           t           e                                      u
    d       u           a           s                                      d
    v       d           n       9p  r   o   m  10p  t  11i  n   g           i
    i       o           d           o           a       n                  n
   12s  e   l   e   c   t   i   n   g           r       s                  g
    i       i           n           d           a       u
    n       s           g           i           p       l
    g       t                       n           h       a
            13h e   a   r   i   n   g           r       t
            n                                   a       e
           14i  n   s   e   n   s   i   t   i   v   e   d
            n                                   s
            g                      15d  e   f   e   n   s   i   v   e
                                                g
```

TRUE/FALSE

1. T	**3.** F	**5.** T	**7.** F	**9.** T
2. F	**4.** T	**6.** F	**8.** F	**10.** T

COMPLETION

1. conversational narcissist
2. sincere question
3. residual message
4. shift-response
5. counterfeit question
6. constructive criticism
7. diversion
8. praise
9. reassurance
10. agreement

MULTIPLE CHOICE

1. f		**7.** a		**13.** b		**19.** e		**25.** a
2. g		**8.** g		**14.** a		**20.** c		**26.** d
3. c		**9.** b		**15.** g		**21.** c		**27.** a
4. d		**10.** f		**16.** c		**22.** a		**28.** c
5. b		**11.** d		**17.** f		**23.** c		**29.** b
6. a		**12.** e		**18.** d		**24.** d		**30.** d

Chapter 8

Communication and Relational Dynamics

OUTLINE

Use this outline to take notes as you read the chapter in the text or as your instructor lectures in class.

I. Why we form relationships

A. Attraction
1. Similarity and complementarity
2. Reciprocal attraction
3. Competence
4. Disclosure
5. Proximity

B. Intimacy
1. The dimensions of intimacy
   a. Physical
   b. Intellectual
   c. Emotional
   d. Shared activities
2. Masculine and feminine intimacy styles
   a. Self-disclosure
   b. Shared activities

3. Cultural influences on intimacy
   a. Historical
   b. Cultural
      1) Class/group
      2) Collectivist
      3) Individualist

4. The limits of intimacy

C. Rewards–Social exchange theory
1. Outcomes
2. Comparison level
3. Comparison level of alternatives

II. Models of relational development and maintenance

A. Developmental Models

1. Initiating
2. Experimenting
3. Intensifying
4. Integrating
5. Bonding
6. Differentiating
7. Circumscribing
8. Stagnating
9. Avoiding
10. Terminating

B. Dialectical Perspectives

1. Dialectical tensions
   a. Connection vs. autonomy
   b. Predictability vs. novelty
   c. Openness vs. privacy
2. Strategies for managing dialectical tensions
   a. Denial
   b. Disorientation
   c. Selection
   d. Alternation
   e. Segmentation
   f. Moderation
   g. Reframing
   h. Reaffirmation

C. Chracteristics of Relational Development and Maintenance

1. Relationships are constantly changing
2. Movement is always to a new place

III. Self-disclosure in relationships

A. Definition

1. Deliberate
2. Significant
3. Not known by others

B. Degrees of Self-Disclosure

1. Social penetration model: Breadth and depth
2. Types: Clichés, facts, opinions, feelings

C. A Model of Self-Disclosure: Open, Hidden, Blind, Unknown

D. Characteristics of Self-Disclosure

1. Usually occurs in dyads
2. Occurs incrementally
3. Few transactions involve high levels
4. Relatively scarce
5. Usually occurs in positive relationships

Harcourt Brace & Company

E. **Reasons for Self-Disclosure**
   1. Catharsis
   2. Self-clarification
   3. Self-validation
   4. Reciprocity
   5. Identity management
   6. Relationship maintenance and enhancement
   7. Social control
   8. Manipulation

F. **Guidelines for Self-Disclosure**
   1. Consider the Importance of the Other Person
   2. Evaluate the Risks Involved
   3. Make the Disclosure Relevant to the Situation at Hand
   4. Make the Amount and Type of Self-Disclosure Appropriate
   5. Consider Constructive Effects
   6. Make the Disclosure Clear and Understandable
   7. Reciprocate Disclosure as Appropriate

IV. Alternatives to self-disclosure

A. **Lying**
   1. White lies
   2. Reasons for lying
      a. Save face
      b. Avoid tension/conflict
      c. Guide social interaction
      d. Expand/reduce relationships
      e. Gain power
   3. Effects of lies - threats to the relationship

B. **Equivocal Language**
   1. Spares embarrassment
   2. Less stressful
   3. Saves face
   4. Saves speaker from being caught lying

C. **Hinting**
   1. Saves receiver from embarrassment
   2. Saves sender from embarrassment

D. **The Ethics of Evasion**

KEY TERMS

Use these key terms to review major concepts from your text. Write the definition for each key term in the space to the right.

alternation _____

attraction _____

avoiding _____

bonding _____

breadth _____

catharsis _____

circumscribing _____

clichés _____

comparison level _____

comparison level of alternatives _____

connection-autonomy dialectic _____

denial _____

depth _____

dialectical tensions _____

differentiating _____

disorientation _____

emotional intimacy _____

equivocal language _____

experimenting _____

facts _____

feelings _____

hinting _____

identity management _____

initiating _____

integrating _____

intellectual intimacy _____

intensifying _____

Harcourt Brace & Company

intimacy _____

Johari Window _____

lying _____

manipulation _____

moderation _____

openness-privacy dialectic _____

opinions _____

physical intimacy _____

predictability-novelty dialectic _____

proximity _____

reaffirmation _____

reciprocal attraction _____

reciprocity _____

reframing _____

relational enhancement _____

relational maintenance _____

rewards _____

segmentation _____

selection _____

self-clarification _____

self-disclosure _____

self-validation _____

similarity _____

small talk _____

social control _____

Harcourt Brace & Company

social exchange theory _____

social penetration _____

stages of relationships _____

stagnating _____

terminating _____

uncertainty reduction _____

white lie _____

Harcourt Brace & Company

ACTIVITIES

8.1 DISCOVERING DIALECTICS

◆ Activity Type: Invitation to Insight

PURPOSE

To identify and describe behaviors that contribute to dialectical tensions in relationships.

INSTRUCTIONS

1. Identify the dialectical tensions operating in the situations below, taking time to explain the conflicting feelings and thoughts in each.
2. Identify one or more of the eight strategies for managing dialectical tensions (denial, disorientation, selection, alternation, segmentation, moderation, reframing and reaffirmation) that you believe would be most beneficial to the relationship, and explain how the relationship would deal with the dialectical tension under these circumstances.
3. Describe dialectical tensions at work in your own relationships and label and explain the strategies that you use to deal with them.

SITUATION	DIALECTICAL TENSION	STRATEGY FOR MANAGING
Example Sandra, 19, and her mother, Tracy, have become good friends over the past few years. Sandra now has a serious boyfriend and spends less time talking to her mother.	The openness-privacy dialectic is probably at work here. Sandra and Tracy continue to share the intimacy of their mother-daughter relationship, but privacy needs about the boyfriend probably keep them at more distance.	Sandra and Tracy are likely to use the segmentation strategy, in which they maintain openness about many areas, but keep certain parts of the boyfriend relationship "off limits."

Harcourt Brace & Company

SITUATION	DIALECTICAL TENSION	STRATEGY FOR MANAGING
1. Daryl is new to the software firm where Steve has been for five years. Daryl has asked Steve to play golf this weekend. Steve is uncomfortable about mixing business and pleasure, but still wants to have a good working relationship with Daryl.		
2. Nesto and Gina have been dating for 6 months. They continue to enjoy one another's company, but both of them have begun to notice annoying little habits that the other one has.		
3. Jenner and A.J. are siblings who have always relied on one another completely. Jenner appreciates A.J.'s dependability, but wishes their relationship wasn't so boring.		
4. Eugenia and Shane have worked at the same business for 20 years. They have collaborated on a number of projects. They've tried to get together socially, but Eugenia's husband and Shane's wife don't seem to get along.		

Harcourt Brace & Company

SITUATION	DIALECTICAL TENSION	STRATEGY FOR MANAGING
5. Christina and Nicole are roommates. Christina wants them to share everything, but Nicole is not proud of a few things she's done and doesn't want to face her friend's judgment.		
6. Your example:		
7. Your example:		
8. Your example:.		

Harcourt Brace & Company

8.2 BREADTH AND DEPTH OF RELATIONSHIPS

◆ Activity Type: Invitation to Insight

PURPOSES

1. To help you understand the breadth and depth of a relationship that is important to you.
2. To help you decide if you are satisfied with the breadth and depth of that relationship, and possibly to modify it.

INSTRUCTIONS

1. Use the form below to make a social penetration model for a significant relationship you have, indicating the depth and breadth of various areas. See Figure 8.5 and 8.6 in Chapter 8 of *Looking Out/Looking In* for an example of the social penetration model.
2. Answer the questions at the end of the exercise.

SOCIAL PENETRATION MODEL

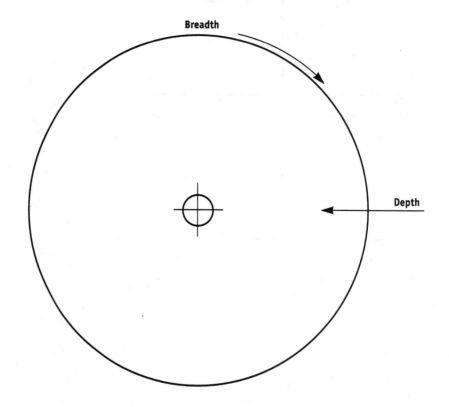

Significant relationship described:

CONCLUSIONS

How deep or shallow is your relationship with this person?

_____

_____

Does the depth vary from one area (breadth) to another? In what way?

_____

_____

_____

Are you satisfied with the depth and breadth of this relationship?

_____

_____

_____

What could you do to change the relationship?

_____

_____

_____

_____

_____

_____

_____

8.3 REASONS FOR NONDISCLOSURE*

◆ Activity Type: Invitation to Insight

PURPOSE

To give you an idea of the reasons you do not disclose and the rationality of these reasons.

INSTRUCTIONS

1. Choose a particular individual about whom you want to analyze your self-disclosing behavior.
2. In the column to the left of each item, indicate the extent to which you use each reason to avoid disclosing.

   5 = almost always   2 = rarely
   4 = often   1 = never
   3 = sometimes

3. In the column to the right of each item, indicate how reasonable and realistic the reason is.

   5 = totally realistic
   4 = mostly realistic
   3 = partly realistic, partly unrealistic
   2 = mostly unrealistic
   1 = totally unrealistic

HOW FREQUENTLY DO YOU USE THE REASON?		HOW REALISTIC AND RATIONAL IS THE REASON?
_____	1. I can't find the opportunity to self-disclose with this person.	_____
_____	2. If I disclose I might hurt the other person.	_____
_____	3. If I disclose I might be evaluating or judging the person.	_____
_____	4. I can't think of topics that I would disclose.	_____
_____	5. Self-disclosure would give information that might be used against me at some time.	_____
_____	6. If I disclose it might cause me to make personal changes.	_____

*Based on a survey developed by Lawrence B. Rosenfeld, "Self-Disclosure Avoidance: Why Am I Afraid to Tell You Who I Am?" *Communication Monographs* 46 (1979): 63–74.

**HOW FREQUENTLY
DO YOU USE
THE REASON?**

**HOW REALISTIC
AND RATIONAL
IS THE REASON?**

_____ 7. Self-disclosure might threaten relationships I have with people other than the close acquaintance to whom I disclose. _____

_____ 8. Self-disclosure is a sign of weakness. _____

_____ 9. If I disclose I might lose control over the other person. _____

_____ 10. If I disclose I might discover I am less than I wish to be. _____

_____ 11. If I disclose I might project an image I do not want to project. _____

_____ 12. If I disclose the other person might not understand what I was saying. _____

_____ 13. If I disclose the other person might evaluate me negatively. _____

_____ 14. Self-disclosure is a sign of some emotional disturbance. _____

_____ 15. Self-disclosure might hurt our relationship. _____

_____ 16. I am afraid that self-disclosure might lead to an intimate relationship with the other person. _____

_____ 17. Self-disclosure might threaten my physical safety. _____

_____ 18. If I disclose I might give information that makes me appear inconsistent. _____

_____ 19. Any other reasons: _____ _____

What does this personal survey tell you about your thoughts and feelings about self-disclosure with this person?

_____

_____

_____

Do you think your level of self-disclosure is appropriate or inappropriate with this person? Why?

_____

_____

_____

8.4 DEGREES OF SELF-DISCLOSURE

◆ Activity Type: Invitation to Insight

PURPOSES

1. To demonstrate that self-disclosure can operate on a variety of levels, some quite intimate and others less revealing.
2. To give you practice in applying various types of self-disclosure to personal situations.

INSTRUCTIONS

For each of the following topics, write two statements for each level of self-disclosure. (See Chapter 8 of *Looking Out/Looking In* for descriptions of each level.)

Example

Topic: School

1. Clichés
   a. *These exams sure are a drag!*
   b. *Textbooks sure are expensive!*

2. Facts
   a. *I'm a psychology major at the University of Oregon.*
   b. *I'm getting a teaching certificate so I'll be able to teach social studies.*

3. Opinions
   a. *I believe in affirmative action but I don't think there should be quotas for women and minorities.*
   b. *I don't think instructors should count class participation as part of a person's grade.*

4. Feelings
   a. *I feel scared when I think about the future. I'm almost finished with four years of college, and I'm still confused about what to do with my life.*
   b. *I get angry when Professor Autel doesn't prepare for our class.*

TOPIC: MY FAMILY

1. Clichés

   a. _____

   b. _____

2. Facts

   a. _____

   b. _____

3. Opinions

   a. _____

   b. _____

4. Feelings

   a. _____

   b. _____

TOPIC: MY CAREER PLANS

1. Clichés

   a. _____

   b. _____

2. Facts

   a. _____

   b. _____

3. Opinions

   a. _____

   b. _____

4. Feelings

   a. _____

   b. _____

TOPIC: MY FRIENDSHIPS

1. Clichés

   a. _____

   b. _____

2. Facts

   a. _____

   b. _____

3. Opinions

   a. _____

   b. _____

4. Feelings

   a. _____

   b. _____

TOPIC: SPORTS

1. Clichés

   a. _____

   b. _____

2. Facts

   a. _____

   b. _____

3. Opinions

   a. _____

   b. _____

4. Feelings

   a. _____

   b. _____

Harcourt Brace & Company

8.5 RESPONSES IN RELATIONSHIPS

❖ Activity Type: Skill Builder

PURPOSES

1. To generate responses to relational situations.
2. To evaluate the effectiveness and ethics of each situation.

INSTRUCTIONS

1. In groups, use the situations described below to record your possible words for each type of response listed.
2. Evaluate the effectiveness and ethics of your response.
3. Record an example of a situation of your own.

Example

Your friend asks you if you had a good time when you went out with his cousin last night.

Self-disclosure *I didn't have a great time, but then we were just getting to know one another. I don't think we had much in common.*

Partial disclosure *I had fun when we went to the movie.*

White lie or lie *Your cousin was a lot of fun and the movie was great.*

Hinting or equivocation *First dates are really times of discovery, aren't they?*

Which response is most effective/which most ethical? *I think the white lie was the most effective here. While I wasn't exactly truthful with my friend, I just don't want to tell him how boring I think his cousin is. I think it is better to just be nice to him and his cousin. Then both of them can save face, too.*

1. A family member calls and asks how you are doing in classes.

   Self-disclosure _____

   _____

   Partial disclosure _____

   _____

   White lie or lie _____

   _____

   Hinting or equivocation _____

   _____

Harcourt Brace & Company

Which responses are most effective/which most ethical? _____

_____

_____

2. You are applying to rent an apartment that prohibits animals. You have a cat.

Self-disclosure _____

_____

Partial disclosure _____

_____

White lie or lie _____

_____

Hinting or equivocation _____

_____

Which responses are most effective/which most ethical? _____

_____

_____

3. You are being interviewed by a group of people to rent a room in the house they live in. They want to know if you are loud, clean, responsible, and the like.

Self-disclosure _____

_____

Partial disclosure _____

_____

White lie or lie _____

_____

Hinting or equivocation _____

_____

Harcourt Brace & Company

Which responses are most effective/which most ethical? _____

_____

_____

4. Your roommates ask what you think of the bright posters they've just put up around the room.

Self-disclosure _____

_____

Partial disclosure _____

_____

_____

White lie or lie _____

_____

Hinting or equivocation_____

_____

Which responses are most effective/which most ethical? _____

_____

_____

5. Your romantic partner asks how many other people you've really loved before you met him or her.

Self-disclosure _____

_____

Partial disclosure _____

_____

White lie or lie _____

_____

Hinting or equivocation_____

_____

Which responses are most effective/which most ethical? _____

_____

_____

6. Your very opinionated father asks what you think of the people running for political office.

Self-disclosure _____

_____

Partial disclosure _____

_____

White lie or lie_____

_____

Hinting or equivocation_____

_____

Which responses are most effective/which most ethical? _____

_____

_____

7. Your boss at work wants to know what your plans for the future are.

Self-disclosure_____

_____

Partial disclosure _____

_____

White lie or lie_____

_____

Harcourt Brace & Company

Hinting or equivocation_____

_____

Which responses are most effective/which most ethical? _____

_____

_____

8. Your mother asks you what your brother/sister has been up to lately.

Self-disclosure _____

_____

Partial disclosure _____

_____

White lie or lie_____

_____

Hinting or equivocation_____

_____

Which responses are most effective/which most ethical? _____

_____

_____

9. Your romantic partner wants to know why you are spending so much time with your other friends.

Self-disclosure _____

_____

Partial disclosure _____

_____

White lie or lie_____

_____

Hinting or equivocation_____

_____

Which responses are most effective/which most ethical? _____

_____

_____

10. Your example _____

_____

Self-disclosure_____

_____

Partial disclosure _____

_____

White lie or lie_____

_____

Hinting or equivocation_____

_____

Which responses are most effective/which most ethical? _____

_____

_____

Harcourt Brace & Company

8.6 RELATIONAL STAGES AND SELF-DISCLOSURE

❖ Activity Type: Skill Builder

PURPOSES

1. To analyze different degrees of self-disclosure.
2. To discuss the appropriate levels of self-disclosure for different relational stages.

INSTRUCTIONS

1. In a group discuss the various situations listed below.
2. Identify the type of response that is likely (equivocation, lies, hinting, disclosure–include level such as fact or feeling).
3. Determine the function that response serves in the relationship.
4. Identify the relational stage(s) that may be illustrated by this type of response.

Example

Two friends are discussing the effects of divorce in their families.
Type(s) of responses likely *Self-disclosure is likely to occur in this situation. Because they have similar experiences, the likelihood of reciprocity of self-disclosure is high. It will probably come from the highest levels of self-disclosure, feelings, but might also include a number of facts.*
Function in relationship *The self-disclosure functions to maintain the relationship, to increase intellectual and emotional intimacy, and to advance the stage of the relationship.*
Relational stage illustrated *This type of self-disclosure would most likely occur in an intensifying stage of a relationship, where the friends have gone beyond the small talk of experimenting and are beginning to develop more trust, more depth rather than breadth of self-disclosure, and where secrets are told and favors given.*

1. Friends are telling one another about their use of/refusal to use drugs.

   Type(s) of responses likely _____

   _____

   Function in relationship _____

   _____

   Relational stage illustrated _____

   _____

Harcourt Brace & Company

2. Two classmates are comparing their grades.

Type(s) of responses likely _____

_____

Function in relationship _____

_____

Relational stage illustrated _____

_____

3. A boyfriend and girlfriend are telling one another about their past romantic involvements.

Type(s) of responses likely _____

_____

Function in relationship _____

_____

Relational stage illustrated _____

_____

4. Two friends are shopping for clothes and giving one another advice on what looks good/bad.

Type(s) of responses likely _____

_____

Function in relationship _____

_____

Relational stage illustrated _____

_____

5. A parent asks a 20-year-old about his or her weekend.

Type(s) of responses likely _____

_____

Function in relationship _____

_____

Relational stage illustrated _____

_____

6. A manager and employee have agreed to sit down and talk about the problems they are experiencing with each other.

Type(s) of responses likely _____

_____

Function in relationship _____

_____

Relational stage illustrated _____

_____

7. A friend has just experienced a death in the family and the partner is expressing concern.

Type(s) of responses likely _____

_____

Function in relationship _____

_____

Relational stage illustrated _____

_____

8. Two acquaintances are exchanging their attitudes toward marriage.

Type(s) of responses likely _____

_____

Function in relationship _____

_____

Relational stage illustrated _____

_____

9. Two women are discussing childbearing.

Type(s) of responses likely _____

_____

Function in relationship _____

_____

Relational stage illustrated _____

_____

10. Two friends are discussing their worries and feelings of responsibility regarding their parents' advancing age.

Type(s) of responses likely _____

_____

Function in relationship _____

_____

Relational stage illustrated _____

_____

Harcourt Brace & Company

CROSSWORD PUZZLE

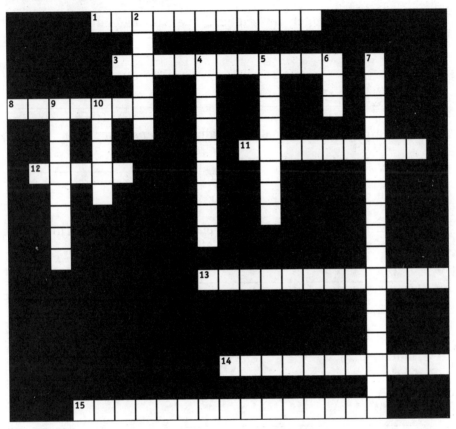

Across

1 a motivation for self-disclosing based on the research evidence that individuals disclosing information about themselves encourage others to self-disclose in return

3 tensions that exist when two opposing or incompatible forces exist simultaneously in a relationship

8 first dimension of self-disclosure involving the range of subjects being discussed

11 speech that focuses on building beginning relationships, usually focusing on similarities with the other person

12 a lie that is a deliberate hiding or misrepresentation of the truth, intended to help, or not to harm, the receiver

13 an act of self-disclosure calculated in advance to achieve a desired result

14 the reduction process of getting to know others by gaining more information about them

15 confirmation of a belief you hold about yourself

Down

2 a ritualized, stock statement delivered in response to a social situation

4 ambiguous language that has two or more equally plausible meanings

5 a state of personal sharing arising from physical, intellectual, or emotional contact

6 a deliberate attempt to hide or misrepresent the truth

7 a model that describes relationships in terms of their breadth and depth

9 a semieconomic theory of relationships that suggests we often seek out people who can give us rewards greater than or equal to the costs we encounter.

10 a dimension of self-disclosure involving a shift from relatively nonrevealing messages to more personal ones

TRUE/FALSE

Mark the statements below as true or false. Correct statements that are false on the lines below to create a true statement.

_____ **1.** Intimacy is definitely rewarding, so maximizing intimacy is the best way of relating to others.

_____

_____

_____ **2.** The level of intimacy that feels right can change over time.

_____

_____

_____ **3.** Research shows that male-male relationships involve less disclosure than male-female or female-female relationships.

_____

_____

_____ **4.** Women are better at developing and maintaining intimate relationships than men.

_____

_____

_____ **5.** Germans and Japanese are more disclosing than members of any culture studied.

_____

_____

_____ **6.** The struggle to achieve important, but seemingly incompatible goals in relationships, results in the creation of dialectical tension.

_____

_____

_____ **7.** The struggle between independence and dependence in a relationship is called the openness-privacy dialectic.

_____

_____

_____ **8.** Intimacy is not the only goal of relationships.

_____

_____

_____ **9.** Research indicates that partners in intimate relationships engage in high levels of self-disclosure frequently.

_____

_____

_____ **10.** People justify over half of their lies as ways to avoid embarrassment for themselves or others.

_____

_____

COMPLETION

Fill in the blanks below with the correct terms chosen from the list below.

open	hidden	blind	unknown	intellectual
physical	emotional	catharsis	hinting	attraction variable

1. _____ is the type of intimacy that comes from an exchange of important ideas.

2. _____ is the type of intimacy that comes from touching, struggling, or sex.

3. _____ is the type of intimacy that comes from exchanging important feelings.

4. _____ is an explanation for what makes us want to develop personal relationships with some people and not with others.

5. _____ is a motivation for self-disclosing that allows you to "get it off your chest," to relieve yourself of uncomfortable secrecy.

6. _____ is a frame of the Johari Window that consists of information that you know about yourself but aren't willing to reveal to others.

7. _____ is a frame of the Johari Window that consists of information of which neither you nor the other person is aware.

8. _____ is a frame of the Johari Window that consists of information of which both you and the other person are aware.

9. _____ is a frame of the Johari Window that consists of information of which you are unaware but the other person in the relationship knows.

10. _____ is an alternative to self-disclosure in which the person gives only a clue to the direct meaning of the response.

MULTIPLE CHOICE

Place the letter of the developmental stage of the intimate relationship on the line before its example found below.

a. initiating
b. experimenting
c. intensifying
d. integrating
e. bonding

f. differentiating
g. circumscribing
h. stagnating
i. avoiding
j. terminating

_____ 1. A public ritual marks this stage.

_____ 2. First glances and "sizing up" each other typifies this stage.

_____ 3. Called the "we" stage, this stage involves increasing self-disclosure.

_____ 4. Lots of "small talk" typifies this stage.

_____ 5. This stage involves much focus on individual rather than dyadic interests.

_____ 6. There's very little growth or experimentation in this stage.

_____ 7. This stage involves much behavior that talks around the relational issues because the partners expect bad feelings.

_____ 8. The partners' social circles merge at this stage and they make purchases or commitments together.

_____ 9. No attempts are made to contact the other at this stage.

_____ 10. The relationship is redefined or dissolved at this stage.

_____ 11. A marriage ceremony would be typical here.

_____ 12. Roommates who make sure they are never in the same room and who are tolerating one another only until the lease is up might be at this stage.

_____ **13.** A couple who avoids talking about future commitment because they are afraid of how the discussion will go is probably at this state.

_____ **14.** This stage represents most communication at a social gathering where people are just getting to know one another.

_____ **15.** In this stage, people spend an increasing amount of time together, asking for support from one another and doing favors for one another.

CROSSWORD PUZZLE

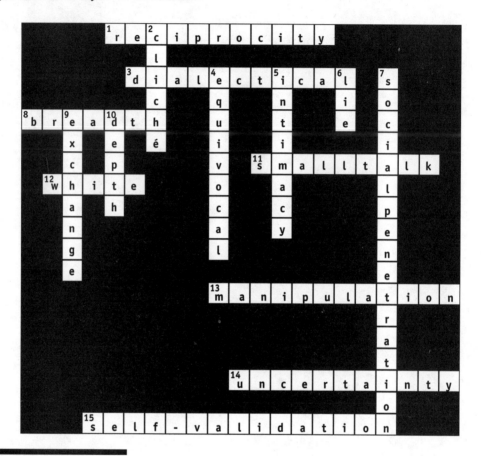

TRUE/FALSE

1. F	**3.** T	**5.** F	**7.** F	**9.** F
2. T	**4.** F	**6.** T	**8.** T	**10.** T

COMPLETION

1. intellectual	**5.** catharsis	**9.** blind
2. physical	**6.** hidden	**10.** hinting
3. emotional	**7.** unknown	
4. attraction variable	**8.** open	

MULTIPLE CHOICE

1. e	**4.** b	**7.** g	**10.** j	**13.** g
2. a	**5.** f	**8.** d	**11.** e	**14.** b
3. c	**6.** h	**9.** i	**12.** i	**15.** c

Chapter 9

Improving Communication Climates

OUTLINE

Use this outline to take notes as you read the chapter in the text and/or as your instructor lectures in class.

I. Communication climate: The key to positive relationships

A. Confirming Communication
1. Recognition
2. Acknowledgment
3. Endorsement

B. Disconfirming Communication
1. Verbal abuse
2. Complaining
3. Impervious responses
4. Interrupting
5. Irrelevant responses
6. Tangential responses
7. Impersonal responses
8. Ambiguous responses
9. Incongruous responses

C. How Communication Climates Develop
1. Escalatory conflict spirals
2. De-escalatory conflict spirals

II. Defensiveness: Causes and remedies

A. Causes: Face-Threatening Acts

B. Types of Defensive Reactions
1. Attacking the critic
   a. Verbal aggression
   b. Sarcasm
2. Distorting critical information
   a. Rationalization
   b. Compensation
   c. Regression

3. Avoiding dissonant information
   a. Physical avoidance
   b. Repression
   c. Apathy
   d. Displacement

C. **Preventing Defensiveness in Others**
   1. Evaluation versus description
   2. Control versus problem orientation
   3. Strategy versus spontaneity
   4. Neutrality versus empathy
   5. Superiority versus equality
   6. Certainty versus provisionalism

D. **Responding Nondefensively to Criticism**
   1. Seek more information
      a. Ask for specifics
      b. Guess about specifics
      c. Paraphrase the speaker's ideas
      d. Ask what the critic wants
      e. Ask what else is wrong
   2. Agree with the critic
      a. Agree with the facts
      b. Agree with the critic's perception

KEY TERMS

Use these key terms to review major concepts from your text. Write the definition for each key term in the space to the right.

acknowledgment _____

ambiguous response _____

apathy _____

certainty _____

cognitive dissonance _____

communication climate _____

compensation _____

complaining _____

confirming communication _____

controlling communication _____

Harcourt Brace & Company

de-escalatory conflict spiral _____

defense mechanism _____

defensiveness _____

descriptive communication _____

disconfirming communication _____

displacement _____

empathy _____

endorsement _____

equality _____

escalatory conflict spiral _____

evaluative communication _____

face-threatening act _____

Gibb categories _____

impersonal response _____

impervious response _____

incongruous response _____

interrupting _____

irrelevant response _____

neutrality _____

physical avoidance _____

problem orientation _____

provisionalism _____

rationalization _____

recognition _____

regression _____

Harcourt Brace & Company

repression _____

sarcasm_____

spiral _____

spontaneity_____

strategy _____

superiority _____

tangential response _____

verbal abuse _____

verbal aggression _____

Harcourt Brace & Company

ACTIVITIES

9.1 UNDERSTANDING YOUR DEFENSIVE RESPONSES

◆ Activity Type: Invitation to Insight

PURPOSE

To help you identify your typical defensive responses.

INSTRUCTIONS

1. Identify the person or people who would be most likely to deliver each of the following critical messages to you. If you are unlikely to hear one or more of the following messages, substitute a defensiveness-arousing topic of your own.
2. For each situation, describe
   a. the person likely to deliver the message.
   b. the typical content of the message.
   c. the general type of response(s) you make: attacking, distorting, or avoiding.
   d. your typical verbal response(s).
   e. your typical nonverbal response(s).
   f. the part of your presenting self being defended.
   g. the probable consequences of these response(s).

Example

A negative comment about your use of time.
Person likely to deliver this message *my parents*
Typical content of the message *wasting my time watching TV instead of studying*
General type(s) of response *attacking, distorting*
Your typical verbal response(s) *"Get off my back! I work hard! I need time to relax." "I'll study later; I've got plenty of time."*
Your typical nonverbal response(s) *harsh tone of voice, sullen silence for an hour or two*
Part of presenting self being defended *good student, not lazy*
Probable consequences of your response(s) *uncomfortable silence, more criticism from parents in the future*

1. Negative comment about your appearance.

   Person likely to deliver this message _____

Typical content of the message _____

_____

General type(s) of response _____

Your typical verbal response(s)_____

_____

Your typical nonverbal response(s) _____

_____

Part(s) of presenting self being defended _____

Probable consequences of your response(s) _____

_____

_____

2. Criticism about your choice of friends.

Person likely to deliver this message_____

Typical content of the message _____

_____

General type(s) of response _____

Your typical verbal response(s)_____

_____

Your typical nonverbal response(s) _____

_____

Part(s) of presenting self being defended _____

Probable consequences of your response(s) _____

_____

_____

3. Criticism of a job you've just completed.

Person likely to deliver this message _____

Typical content of the message _____

_____

General type(s) of response _____

Your typical verbal response(s) _____

_____

Your typical nonverbal response(s) _____

_____

Part(s) of presenting self being defended _____

Probable consequences of your response(s) _____

_____

_____

4. Criticism of your schoolwork.

Person likely to deliver this message _____

Typical content of the message _____

_____

General type(s) of response _____

Your typical verbal response(s) _____

_____

Your typical nonverbal response(s) _____

_____

Part(s) of presenting self being defended _____

Probable consequences of your response(s) _____

_____

_____

5. Criticism of your diet or eating habits.

Person likely to deliver this message _____

Typical content of the message _____

_____

General type(s) of response _____

Your typical verbal response(s) _____

_____

Your typical nonverbal response(s) _____

_____

Part(s) of presenting self being defended _____

Probable consequences of your response(s) _____

_____

_____

6. A negative comment about your exercise (or lack of it).

Person likely to deliver this message _____

Typical content of the message _____

_____

General type(s) of response _____

Your typical verbal response(s) _____

_____

Your typical nonverbal response(s) _____

_____

Part(s) of presenting self being defended _____

Probable consequences of your response(s) _____

_____

_____

9.2 DEFENSIVE AND SUPPORTIVE LANGUAGE

◆❖ Activity Type: Skill Builder

PURPOSE

To help you recognize the difference between the Gibb categories of defensive and supportive language.

INSTRUCTIONS

1. For each of the situations below, write two statements a speaker might make. One should contain evaluative language and the other descriptive language.
2. In the space adjacent to each statement, label the Gibb categories of language that your words represent.

Example

A neighbor's late-night stereo music playing is disrupting your sleep.
Defense-arousing statement *Why don't you show a little consideration and turn that* *damn thing down? If I hear any more noise I'm going to call the police!*
Type(s) of defensive language *evaluation, control*
Supportive statement *When I hear your stereo music late at night I can't sleep, which* *leaves me more and more tired. I'd like to figure out some way you can listen and I can* *sleep.*
Type(s) of supportive language *description, problem orientation*

1. You're an adult child who moves back in with your parents. They say they expect you to follow the "rules of the house."

   Defense-arousing statement _____

   _____

   _____

   _____

   Type(s) of defensive language _____

   Supportive statement _____

   _____

   _____

   _____

   Type(s) of supportive language _____

Harcourt Brace & Company

2. Your roommate tells you you're trying to be "somebody you're not."

Defense-arousing statement _____

_____

_____

_____

Type(s) of defensive language _____

Supportive statement _____

_____

_____

_____

Type(s) of supportive language _____

3. A boss criticizes you for being late to work when you've been having car trouble.

Defense-arousing statement _____

_____

_____

_____

Type(s) of defensive language _____

Supportive statement _____

_____

_____

_____

Type(s) of supportive language _____

4. An elderly in-law who lives across the country calls to tell you what a bad job you're doing raising your child.

Defense-arousing statement _____

_____

_____

_____

Type(s) of defensive language _____

Supportive statement _____

_____

_____

_____

Type(s) of supportive language _____

5. Your friend buys the same thing you did after you bragged about the deal you got.

Defense-arousing statement _____

_____

_____

_____

Type(s) of defensive language _____

Supportive statement _____

_____

_____

_____

Type(s) of supportive language _____

6. On many occasions a friend drops by your place without calling first. Since you often have other plans, this behavior puts you in an uncomfortable position.

Defense-arousing statement _____

_____

_____

_____

Type(s) of defensive language _____

Supportive statement _____

_____

_____

_____

Type(s) of supportive language _____

7. (Record a situation of your own here.) _____

_____

Defense-arousing statement _____

_____

_____

_____

Type(s) of defensive language _____

Supportive statement _____

_____

_____

_____

Type(s) of supportive language _____

Harcourt Brace & Company

9.3 COPING WITH TYPICAL CRITICISM

❖ Activity Type: Skill Builder

PURPOSE

To help you practice nondefensive responses to typical criticisms you may face.

INSTRUCTIONS

1. For each situation below, write a nondefensive response you could use that follows the guidelines of seeking more information or agreeing with the critic described in Chapter 9 of *Looking Out/Looking In*.
2. Join with two partners and identify the members as A, B, and C.
3. Role-play situations 1 and 2 with A responding to the criticisms offered by B, while C uses *9.4 Coping with Criticism* to evaluate A's behavior.
4. Switch roles so that B responds to C's criticisms on items 3 and 4, while A completes the checklist.
5. Switch roles again so that C responds to A's criticisms on items 5 and 6, while B completes the checklist.

SITUATION	HOW I COULD RESPOND EFFECTIVELY TO THE CRITICISM
1. You've been late to work every day this week. Just who do you think you are that you can come wandering in after the rest of us are already working?	
2. This place is a mess! Don't you care about how we live?	
3. No wonder your grades are low. You're always out partying instead of studying.	
4. Your sister got terrific grades this term.	
5. How could you have been so thoughtless at the party last night?	

SITUATION	HOW I COULD RESPOND EFFECTIVELY TO THE CRITICISM
6. It takes you so long to get the idea.	
7. You think I'm your personal servant!	
8. Haven't you finished that yet?	
9. What's the matter with you? You've been so cold lately.	
10. Why can't your children be quiet like theirs?	
11. You should have consulted somebody before acting on that.	
12. Your motivation level sure is low lately.	

9.4 COPING WITH CRITICISM

❖ Activity Type: Oral Skill

PURPOSE

To practice nondefensive responses to criticisms.

INSTRUCTIONS

1. Form triads and identify members as A, B, and C. (OR form dyads, videotape the following, and receive evaluation from your instructor.)
2. Person A describes a common defensiveness-arousing criticism he or she faces, identifying the critic, topic, and the critic's behavior.
3. Person B paraphrases and questions A until he or she understands the critic's behavior.
4. Persons A and B then role-play the situation, with A practicing the skills of seeking more information and agreeing with the critic as described in Chapter 9 of *Looking Out/Looking In.*
5. Person C uses *Coping with Criticism* to evaluate A's skill at responding nondefensively.
6. After the role-play, person C provides feedback to person A.
7. Rotate roles and repeat steps 1–6 until both B and C have had the chance to practice responding nondefensively to criticism.
8. On a separate page, write a thoughtful, realistically complete assessment of how you used the skills for coping with criticism here, and how you could apply these skills in everyday life.

CHECKLIST

5 = Superior   4 = Excellent   3 = Good   2 = Fair   1 = Poor

Seeks additional information to understand criticism and critic

    –asks for specific details of criticism   _____

    –guesses about specific details when critic does not supply facts   _____

    –paraphrases critic to clarify criticism and draw out more information   _____

    –asks what the critic wants   _____

    –asks critic to describe the consequences of behavior
("How does my behavior [be specific] cause problems for you?")   _____

    –asks what else is wrong   _____

Agrees as appropriate with criticism

    –agrees with facts (truth only)

    –agrees with critic's right to perceive event differently
    ("I can understand why it looks that way to you because . . .")   _____

Verbal and nonverbal behaviors   _____

    –voice   _____

    –facial expression   _____

    –posture and gestures   _____

    –body orientation and distance   _____

                   Total   _____

Harcourt Brace & Company

CROSSWORD PUZZLE

Across

2 a disconfirming response with more than one meaning, leaving the other party unsure of the responder's position

4 a defense mechanism in which a person stresses a strength in one area to camouflage a shortcoming in some other area

6 a disconfirming response that ignores another person's attempt to communicate

8 the emotional tone of a relationship between two or more individuals

10 communication messages that express caring or respect for another person

Down

1 a cognitive inconsistency between two conflicting pieces of information, attitudes or behavior

2 a defense mechanism in which a person avoids admitting emotional pain by pretending not to care about an event

3 a disconfirming response that implicitly or explicitly attributes responsibility for the speaker's displeasure to another party

5 a disconforming response in which one communicator breaks into the other's communication

7 communication messages that express a lack of caring or respect for another person

9 a defense mechanism in which a person vents hostile or aggressive feelings on a target that cannot strike back, instead of on the true target

10 communication in which the sender tries to impose some sort of outcome on the receiver, usually resulting in a defensive reaction

11 a disconfirming response that is superficial or trite

TRUE/FALSE

Mark the statements below as true or false. Correct statements that are false on the lines below to create a true statement.

_____ 1. The tone or climate of a relationship is shaped by the degree to which the people believe themselves to be valued by one another.

_____ 2. Disagreeing with another person is always disconfirming or defense-arousing.

_____ 3. Most experts agree that it is psychologically healthier to have someone ignore you than disagree with you.

_____ 4. Both positive and negative communication spirals have their limits; they rarely go on indefinitely.

_____ 5. When the criticism leveled at us is accurate, we will not get defensive.

_____ 6. Communicators strive to resolve inconsistencies or conflicting pieces of information because this "dissonant" condition is uncomfortable.

_____ 7. Using Jack Gibb's supportive behaviors will eliminate defensiveness in your receivers.

_____ 8. According to your text, spontaneity can sometimes be used as a strategy.

_____ 9. When you truly understand hostile comments, you just naturally accept them.

_____ 10. In order to cope with criticism, you should agree with all the critics' statements.

COMPLETION

The Gibb categories of defensive and supportive behavior are six sets of contrasting styles of verbal and nonverbal behavior. Each set describes a communication style that is likely to arouse defensiveness and a contrasting style that is likely to prevent or reduce it. Fill in the blanks with the Gibb behavior described chosen from the list below.

evaluation   description   control   problem orientation   strategy
spontaneity   neutrality   empathy   superiority   equality
certainty   provisionalism

1. _____ is the attitude behind messages that dogmatically imply that the speaker's position is correct and that the other person's ideas are not worth considering.

2. _____ is communication behavior involving messages that describe the speaker's position without evaluating others.

3. _____ is a supportive style of communication in which the communicators focus on working together to solve their problems instead of trying to impose their own solutions on one another.

4. _____ is a defense-arousing style of communication in which the sender tries to manipulate or deceive a receiver.

5. _____ is a supportive style of communication in which the sender expresses a willingness to consider the other person's position.

6. _____ is a defense-arousing style of communication in which the sender states or implies that the receiver is not worthy of respect.

7. _____ is a supportive communication behavior in which the sender expresses a message openly and honestly without any attempt to manipulate the receiver.

8. _____ is a defense-arousing behavior in which the sender expresses indifference toward a receiver.

9. _____ is a defense-arousing message in which the sender tries to impose some sort of outcome on the receiver.

10. _____ is a type of supportive communication that suggests that the sender regards the receiver as worthy of respect.

MULTIPLE CHOICE

Choose the letter of the defensive or supportive category that is best illustrated by each of the situations below.

a. evaluation
b. control
c. strategy
d. neutrality
e. superiority
f. certainty

g. description
h. problem orientation
i. spontaneity
j. empathy
k. equality
l. provisionalism

_____ 1. Gerry insists he has all the facts and needs to hear no more information.

_____ 2. Richard has a strong opinion but will listen to another position.

_____ 3. Lina kept looking at the clock as she was listening to Nan, so Nan thought Lina didn't consider her comments as very important.

_____ 4. "I know Janice doesn't agree with me," Mary said, "but she knows how strongly I feel about this, and I think she understands my position."

_____ 5. "Even though my professor has a Ph.D.," Rosa pointed out, "she doesn't act like she's the only one who knows something; she is really interested in me as a person."

_____ 6. "When I found out that Bob had tricked me into thinking his proposal was my idea so I'd support it, I was really angry."

_____ 7. "Even though we *all* wait tables here, Evanne thinks she's better than any of us—just look at the way she prances around!"

_____ 8. Clara sincerely and honestly told Georgia about her reservations concerning Georgia's planned party.

_____ 9. The co-workers attempted to find a solution to the scheduling issue that would satisfy both of their needs.

_____ 10. "It seems as though my father's favorite phrase is 'I know what's best for you' and that really gripes me."

_____ 11. "You drink too much."

_____ 12. "I was embarrassed when you slurred your speech in front of my boss."

_____ 13. "The flowers and presents are just an attempt to get me to go to bed with him."

_____ 14. "She looked down her nose at me when I told her I didn't exercise regularly."

_____ 15. "Well, if you need more money and I need more help around here, what could we do to make us both happy?"

Choose the letter of the type of coping with criticism that is best illustrated by each of the situations below.

a.   ask for specific details of criticism
b.   guess about specific details
c.   paraphrase to clarify criticism
d.   ask what the critic wants
e.   ask critic to describe the consequences of behavior
f.   ask what else is wrong
g.   agree with true facts
h.   agree with critic's right to perceive differently

Criticism: "You never seem to care about much."

_____ **16.** "Are you referring to my not going to the office party?"

_____ **17.** "You're right that I didn't call you back within 24 hours."

_____ **18.** "What do you want me to care more about?"

_____ **19.** "I can see why you'd be upset with me for not coming to the party because you've told me you want me to be more involved with your work's social events."

_____ **20.** "When I didn't come to the party, were you embarrassed or something?"

_____ **21.** "So not calling you back right away was a problem. Have I upset you any other way?"

_____ **22.** "So you're upset that I'm not visiting you every week, and you think that shows a lack of affection on my part–is that it?"

_____ **23.** "What do you mean?"

_____ **24.** "You're correct in that I couldn't visit this week because of finals."

_____ **25.** "Because I wasn't at the party, it reflected badly on you?"

CROSSWORD PUZZLE

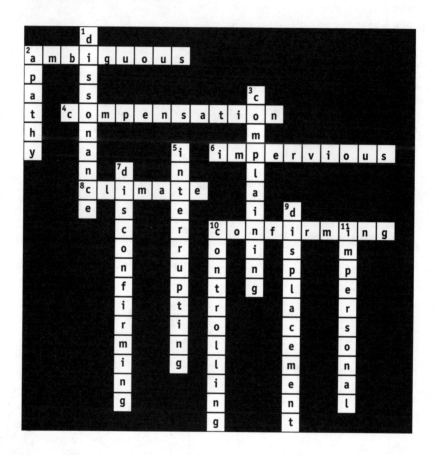

TRUE/FALSE

1. T	3. F	5. F	7. F	9. F
2. F	4. T	6. T	8. T	10. F

COMPLETION

1. certainty
2. description
3. problem orientation
4. strategy
5. provisionalism
6. superiority
7. spontaneity
8. neutrality
9. control
10. equality

MULTIPLE CHOICE

1. f	**6.** c	**11.** a	**16.** b	**21.** f
2. l	**7.** e	**12.** g	**17.** g	**22.** c
3. d	**8.** i	**13.** c	**18.** d	**23.** a
4. j	**9.** h	**14.** e	**19.** h	**24.** g
5. k	**10.** b	**15.** h	**20.** b	**25.** b

Harcourt Brace & Company

Chapter 10

Managing Interpersonal Conflicts

OUTLINE

Use this outline to take notes as you read the chapter in the text and/or as your instructor lectures in class.

I. The nature of conflict

A. Definition
  1. Expressed struggle
  2. Perceived incompatible goals
  3. Perceived scarce rewards
  4. Interdependence
  5. Interference from the other party

B. Conflict Is Natural

C. Conflict Can Be Beneficial

II. Personal conflict styles

A. Nonassertive Behavior
  1. Avoidance
  2. Accommodation

B. Direct Aggression

C. Passive Aggression - "Crazymaking"

D. Indirect Communication

E. Assertion

F. Determining the Best Style
  1. Situation
  2. Receiver
  3. Your goals

III. Assertion without aggression: The clear message format

A. Behavior

B. Interpretation

C. **Feeling**

D. **Consequence**
   1. What happens to you, the speaker
   2. What happens to the person you're addressing
   3. What happens to others

E. **Intention**
   1. Where you stand on an issue
   2. Requests of others
   3. Descriptions of how you plan to act in the future

F. **Using the Clear Message Format**
   1. May be delivered in mixed order
   2. Word to suit your personal style
   3. Combine elements when appropriate
   4. Take your time delivering the message

IV. Conflict in relational systems

A. **Complementary, Symmetrical, and Parallel Styles**

B. **Intimate and Aggressive Styles**

C. **Conflict Rituals**

V. Variables in conflict styles

A. **Gender**

B. **Culture**

VI. Methods of conflict resolution

A. **Win–Lose**

B. **Lose–Lose**

C. **Compromise**

D. **Win–Win**

VII. Win–win communication skills

A. **Identify Your Problem and Unmet Needs**

B. **Make a Date**

C. **Describe Your Problem and Needs**

D. **Consider Your Partner's Point of View**

E. **Negotiate a Solution**
   1. Identify and define the conflict
   2. Generate a number of possible solutions
   3. Evaluate the alternative solutions
   4. Decide on the best solution

F. **Follow Up on the Solution**

VIII. Constructive conflict: Questions and answers

    A. Isn't Win–Win Too Good to Be True?

    B. Isn't Win–Win Too Elaborate?

    C. Isn't Win–Win Negotiating *Too* Rational?

    D. Is It Possible to Change Others?

KEY TERMS

Use these key terms to review major concepts from your text. Write the definition for each key term in the space to the right.

accommodation _____

aggressive conflict style _____

assertion _____

avoidance _____

behavioral description _____

clear message format _____

complementary conflict style _____

compromise_____

conflict _____

conflict ritual _____

consequence statement_____

crazymaking _____

direct aggression _____

feeling statement _____

indirect communication_____

intention statement _____

interdependence_____

interpretation _____

indirect conflict style _____

lose–lose problem solving _____

nonassertion _____

parallel conflict style _____

passive aggression _____

relational conflict style _____

scarce rewards _____

symmetrical conflict style _____

win–lose problem solving _____

win–win problem solving _____

Harcourt Brace & Company

ACTIVITIES

10.1 UNDERSTANDING CONFLICT STYLES

◆❖ Activity Type: Skill Builder

PURPOSE

To help you understand the styles with which conflicts can be handled.

INSTRUCTIONS

1. For each of the conflicts described below, write four responses illustrating nonassertive, directly aggressive, passive aggressive, indirect communication, and assertive communication styles.
2. Describe the probable consequences of each style.

Example

Three weeks ago your friend borrowed an article of clothing, promising to return it soon. You haven't seen it since, and the friend hasn't mentioned it.

Nonassertive response *Say nothing to the friend, hoping she will remember and return the item.*

Probable consequences *There's a good chance I'll never get the item back. I would probably resent the friend and avoid her in the future so I won't have to lend anything else.*

Directly aggressive response *Confront the friend and accuse her of being inconsiderate and irresponsible. Say that she probably ruined the item and is afraid to say so.*

Probable consequences *My friend would get defensive and hurt. Even if she did intentionally keep the item, she'd never admit it when approached this way. We would probably avoid each other in the future.*

Passive aggressive response *Complain to another friend, knowing it will get back to her.*

Probable consequences *My friend might be embarrassed by my gossip and be even more resistant to return it.*

Indirect communication *Drop hints about how I loved to wear the borrowed item. Casually mention how much I hate people who don't return things.*

Probable consequences *My friend might ignore my hints. She'll most certainly resent my roundabout approach, even if she returns the article.*

Assertive response *Confront the friend in a noncritical way and remind her that she still has the item. Ask when she'll return it, being sure to get a specific time.*

Probable consequences *The friend might be embarrassed when I bring the subject up, but since there's no attack it'll probably be okay. Since we'll have cleared up the problem, the relationship can continue.*

1. Someone you've just met at a party criticizes a mutual friend in a way you think is unfair.

   Nonassertive response _____

   _____

   _____

   Probable consequences _____

   _____

   Directly aggressive response _____

   _____

   _____

   Probable consequences _____

   _____

   Passive aggressive response _____

   _____

   _____

   Probable consequences _____

   _____

   Indirect communication _____

   _____

   _____

   Probable consequences _____

   _____

   Assertive response _____

   _____

   _____

   Probable consequences _____

   _____

Harcourt Brace & Company

2. A fan behind you at a ballgame toots a loud air horn every time the home team makes any progress. The noise is spoiling your enjoyment of the game.

Nonassertive response _____

_____

_____

Probable consequences _____

_____

Directly aggressive response_____

_____

_____

Probable consequences _____

_____

Passive aggressive response _____

_____

_____

Probable consequences _____

_____

Indirect communication _____

_____

_____

Probable consequences _____

_____

Assertive response_____

_____

_____

Probable consequences _____

_____

Harcourt Brace & Company

3. Earlier in the day you asked the person with whom you live to stop by the store and pick up snacks for a party you are having this evening. Your roommate arrives home without the food, and it's too late to return to the store.

Nonassertive response _____

_____

_____

Probable consequences _____

_____

Directly aggressive response_____

_____

_____

Probable consequences _____

_____

Passive aggressive response _____

_____

_____

Probable consequences _____

_____

Indirect communication _____

_____

_____

Probable consequences _____

_____

Assertive response_____

_____

_____

_____

Probable consequences _____

_____

4. You are explaining your political views to a friend who has asked your opinion. Now the friend obviously isn't listening. You think to yourself that since the person asked for your ideas, the least he or she can do is pay attention.

Nonassertive response _____

_____

_____

Probable consequences _____

_____

Directly aggressive response_____

_____

_____

Probable consequences _____

_____

Passive aggressive response _____

_____

_____

Probable consequences _____

_____

Indirect communication _____

_____

_____

Probable consequences _____

_____

Assertive response_____

_____

_____

Probable consequences _____

_____

5. You find out that a friend at work told other people with whom you work some very personal information about you.

Nonassertive response _____

_____

_____

Probable consequences _____

_____

Directly aggressive response _____

_____

_____

Probable consequences _____

_____

Passive aggressive response _____

_____

_____

Probable consequences _____

_____

Indirect communication _____

_____

_____

Probable consequences _____

_____

Assertive response _____

_____

_____

Probable consequences _____

_____

Harcourt Brace & Company

10.2 WRITING CLEAR MESSAGES

◆❖ Activity Type: Skill Builder

PURPOSE

To help you turn unclear messages into clear ones.

INSTRUCTIONS

Imagine a situation in which you might have said each of the statements below. Rewrite the messages in the clear message format, being sure to include each of the five elements described in your text.

Example

Unclear message: "It's awful when you can't trust a friend."

Clear message:

Lena, when I gave you the keys to my house so you could borrow those
clothes _____ (behavior)
I figured .you'd know to lock up again when you left. _____ (interpretation)
I was worried and scared _____ (feeling)
because I found the door unlocked and thought there was a break-in. (consequence)
I want to know if you left the house open, and let you know how upset
_I am._ _____ (intention)

1. "Blast it, Robin! Get off my back."

    _____ (behavior)

    _____ (interpretation)

    _____ (feeling)

    _____ (consequence)

    _____ (intention)

2. "I wish you'd pay more attention to me."

_____ (behavior)

_____ (interpretation)

_____ (feeling)

_____ (consequence)

_____ (intention)

3. "You've sure been thoughtful lately."

_____ (behavior)

_____ (interpretation)

_____ (feeling)

_____ (consequence)

_____ (intention)

4. "Nobody's perfect!"

_____ (behavior)

_____ (interpretation)

_____ (feeling)

_____ (consequence)

_____ (intention)

5. "Matt, you're such a slob!"

_____ (behavior)

_____ (interpretation)

_____ (feeling)

_____ (consequence)

_____ (intention)

6. "Let's just forget it; with all the screaming, I get flustered."

_____ (behavior)

_____ (interpretation)

_____ (feeling)

_____ (consequence)

_____ (intention)

7. "I really shouldn't eat any of that cake you baked."

_____ (behavior)

_____ (interpretation)

_____ (feeling)

_____ (consequence)

_____ (intention)

Now list three significant messages that you could send to important people in your life: complaints, requests, or expressions of appreciation. Write them in clear message format.

8. _____ (behavior)

_____ (interpretation)

_____ (feeling)

_____ (consequence)

_____ (intention)

9. _____ (behavior)

_____ (interpretation)

_____ (feeling)

_____ (consequence)

_____ (intention)

Harcourt Brace & Company

10. _____ (behavior)

_____ (interpretation)

_____ (feeling)

_____ (consequence)

_____ (intention)

10.3 YOUR CONFLICT STYLES

◆ Activity Type: Invitation to Insight

PURPOSE

To help you identify the styles you use to handle conflicts.

INSTRUCTIONS

1. Use the form below to record the conflicts that occur in your life. Describe any minor issues which arise as well as major problems.
2. For each incident, describe your conflict style, your approach to resolution, and the consequences of these behaviors.
3. Summarize your findings in the space provided.

INCIDENT	YOUR BEHAVIOR	YOUR CONFLICT STYLE	APPROACH TO RESOLUTION	CONSEQUENCES
Example My friend accused me of being too negative about the possibility of finding rewarding, well-paying work.	I became defensive and angrily denied his claim. In turn I accused him of being too critical.	Direct aggression	Win–lose	After arguing for some time, we left each other, both feeling upset. I'm sure we'll both feel awkward around each other for a while.
1.				
2.				

INCIDENT	YOUR BEHAVIOR	YOUR CONFLICT STYLE	APPROACH TO RESOLUTION	CONSEQUENCES
3.				
4.				
5.				

Harcourt Brace & Company

CONCLUSIONS

Are there any individuals or issues that repeatedly arouse conflicts?

_____

_____

_____

_____

What conflict style(s) do you most commonly use? Do you use different styles with different people or in different situations? Describe.

_____

_____

_____

_____

_____

_____

_____

What approaches do you usually take in resolving conflicts? Do you use different approaches depending on the people or situations? Describe.

_____

_____

_____

What are the consequences of the behaviors you described above? Are you satisfied with them? If not, how could you change?

_____

_____

_____

_____

10.4 THE END VS. THE MEANS

◆❖ Activity Type: Invitation to Insight

PURPOSE

To help you distinguish the ends and the means to those ends in a personal conflict.

INSTRUCTIONS

1. In each of the conflict situations below, identify the <u>ends</u> each party seems to be seeking. There may be ends that the relationship shares as well as individual ends for each of the parties involved. Ends in a conflict are the overall, general (often relational) goals that the dyad has.
2. Brainstorm a series of possible <u>means</u> that could achieve each person's (and the relationship's) ends. Means are the many possible ways to reach the end state.
3. Record conflict situations of your own, identifying ends and means.

CONFLICT SITUATION	SHARED ENDS	SPEAKER'S ENDS	OTHER'S ENDS	POSSIBLE MEANS
Example My friend wants me to visit her in Washington and meet her family. I'd like to visit, but it would cost a lot, and I'd rather save the money for something else.	Shared ends: We both want to maintain the affection in the relationship. We both want one another to know we are important to one another and that we care about one another and our families.	Speaker's ends: I want to spend as little money as possible while still letting my friend know how important she is to me. I don't want to lose her friendship.	Other's ends: She wants to show her family what a good friend I am and have some companionship while she has to stay in Washington.	Possible means: She/her family send me money to go to Washington. We share cost. I combine whatever else I want to do with a short trip to Washington. We arrange for family to meet me when they next come to our city. My friend comes back with her sister or mother to spend time with me.
1. My roommate wants a friend (whom I dislike) to sublease a room in our apartment.				
2. I am dating a person that's of a different race than I am, and my family thinks this is a mistake.				

CONFLICT SITUATION	SHARED ENDS	SPEAKER'S ENDS	OTHER'S ENDS	POSSIBLE MEANS
3. My older sisters think, because of many alcohol problems in our family, that I'll turn into an alcoholic. I tell them not to worry, but they won't get off my back.				
4. My partner thinks I flirt too much.				
5. My mom keeps asking me about my grades and nagging me on the issue of my boyfriend. She thinks I'm going to make the same mistakes as she did.				

CONFLICT SITUATION	SHARED ENDS	SPEAKER'S ENDS	OTHER'S ENDS	POSSIBLE MEANS
6. Some people in my office enjoy listening to country music all the time. I've got nothing against it, but it gets old. I'd like more variety.				
7. My example:				
8. My example:				
9. My example:				

10.5 WIN–WIN PROBLEM SOLVING

◆❖ Activity Type: Invitation to Insight

PURPOSE

To help you apply the win–win problem-solving method to a personal conflict.

INSTRUCTIONS

1. Follow the instructions below as a guide to dealing with an interpersonal conflict facing you now.
2. After completing the no-lose steps, record your conclusions in the space provided.

Step 1: Identify your unmet needs.

_____

_____

_____

_____

Step 2: Make a date. (Choose a time and place that will make it easiest for both parties to work constructively on the issue.)

_____

_____

_____

_____

Step 3: Describe your problem and needs. (Use behavior–interpret–feel–consequence–intend format, but avoid proposing specific means or solutions at this point.)

_____

_____

_____

_____

Step 4: Consider your partner's point of view. (Ask your partner what he or she wants and check your understanding–paraphrase or perception–check as necessary.)

_____

_____

_____

_____

Step 5: Negotiate a solution.

a. Restate the needs of both parties, just to be sure they are clear.

_____

_____

_____

_____

b. Work together to generate a number of possible solutions that might satisfy these needs. Don't criticize any suggestions here!

_____

_____

_____

_____

_____

_____

c. Evaluate the solutions you just listed, considering the advantages and problems of each. If you think of any new solutions, record them above.

_____

_____

_____

d. Decide on the best solution, listing it here.

_____

_____

_____

_____

Step 6: Follow up on the solution. After a trial period, meet with your partner and see if your agreement is satisfying both your needs. If not, return to step 3 and use this procedure to refine your solution.

_____

_____

_____

CONCLUSIONS

In what ways did this procedure differ from the way in which you usually deal with interpersonal conflicts?

_____

_____

_____

Was the outcome of your problem-solving session different from what it might have been if you had communicated in your usual style? How?

_____

_____

_____

In what ways can you use the no-lose methods in your interpersonal conflicts? With whom? On what issues? What kinds of behavior will be especially important?

_____

_____

_____

10.6 CONFLICT RESOLUTION DYADS

❖ Activity Type: Oral Skill

PURPOSE

To develop your skills in using the assertive, win–win conflict resolution methods introduced in Chapter 10 of *Looking Out/Looking In.*

INSTRUCTIONS

1. Join with a partner and discuss conflicts from your lives. Choose one that would be suitable for a win-win conflict attempt. One of you will role-play a real life partner.
2. Engage in the win–win conflict resolution methods introduced in Chapter 10 of *Looking Out/Looking In.* (You may use 10.5 to help you prepare this conflict.)
3. Use the *Checklist* below to evaluate your performance (or videotape the conflict dyad and evaluate one another's performance).
4. On a separate sheet of paper, evaluate your performance in this dyad, and describe how this method can be effectively and realistically applied to everyday conflicts.

CHECKLIST

5 = Superior   4 = Excellent   3 = Good   2 = Fair   1 = Poor

Set a "date" for discussing the issue _____

Describes unmet needs to partner _____
  –other's behavior
  –your interpretations
  –your feelings
  –consequences (for self and/or other)
  –intentions

Seeks verification that partner understands statement of needs _____

Solicits partner's needs, as appropriate _____

Actively listens/perception checks to verify understanding of partner's needs _____

Negotiates win–win solution to best possible extent _____
  –identifies/summarizes conflict
  –generates possible solutions without criticizing
  –evaluates alternatives
  –decides on win–win solution

Plans follow-up meeting to modify solution as necessary. _____

Describes how this method can be applied to everyday conflicts _____

Total _____

CROSSWORD PUZZLE

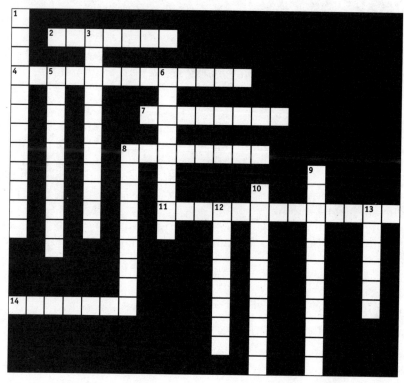

Across

2 an indirect expression of aggression, delivered in a way that allows the sender to maintain a façade of kindness
4 a nonassertive response style in which the communicator submits to a situation rather than attempt to have his or her needs met
7 an expressed struggle between at least two interdependent parties who perceive incompatible goals, scarce rewards, and interference
8 communication that is an oblique way of expressing wants or needs in order to save face for the recipient
11 a relational conflict style in which partners use different but mutually reinforcing behaviors
14 an approach to conflict resolution in which the parties work together to satisfy all their goals

Down

1 the inability to express one's thoughts or feelings when necessary
3 a relational conflict style in which both partners use the same tactics
5 an approach to conflict resolution in which both parties attain at least part of what they wanted through self-sacrifice
6 a nonassertive response style in which the communicator is unwilling to confront a situation in which his or her needs are not being met
8 a statement that describes where the speaker stands on an issue, what he or she wants, or how he or she plans to act in the future
9 a statement that explains the results that follow from either the behavior of the person to whom the message is addressed or from the speaker's interpretation of the addressee's behavior
10 a conflict style that is a pattern of managing disagreements that repeats itself over time in a relationship
12 a relational conflict style in which the approach of the partners varies from one situation to another
13 an unacknowledged repeating pattern of interlocking behavior used by participants in a conflict

Harcourt Brace & Company

TRUE/FALSE

Mark the statements below as true or false. Correct statements that are false on the lines below to create a true statement.

_____ **1.** A conflict can exist only when both parties are aware of a disagreement.

_____

_____ **2.** Conflict will occur only if there is not enough of something (money, love, respect, time, etc.) to go around.

_____

_____ **3.** Very close and compatible relationships will not involve conflict.

_____

_____ **4.** Effective communication during conflicts can actually keep good relationships strong.

_____

_____ **5.** Nonassertion is always a bad idea.

_____

_____ **6.** Verbally abusive couples report significantly less relational satisfaction than do partners who communicate about their conflicts in other ways.

_____

_____ **7.** Satisfied conflict partners tend to make more personal characteristic complaints than behavioral complaints.

_____

_____ **8.** Crazymaking is just another name for passive aggression.

_____

_____ **9.** "It takes two to tango"–in conflict, as in dancing, men and women behave in similar ways.

_____

_____ **10.** The most important cultural factor in shaping attitudes toward conflict is gender.

_____

COMPLETION

Fill in the blanks with the crazymaker term described below.

avoiders   pseudoaccommodators   guiltmakers   subject changers   distracters
mind readers   trivial tyrannizers   gunnysackers   beltliners   trappers

1. _____ don't respond immediately when they get angry. Instead, they let conflicts build up until they all pour out at once.

2. _____ do things they know will irritate their conflict partner rather than honestly sharing their resentments.

3. _____ engage in character analyses, explaining what the other person *really* means, instead of allowing their partners to express feelings honestly.

4. _____ set up a desired behavior for their partners and then when the behavior is met, they attack the very thing they requested.

5. _____ refuse to fight by leaving, falling asleep, or pretending to be busy.

6. _____ try to make their partners feel responsible for causing their pain even though they won't come right out and say what they feel or want.

7. _____ refuse to face up to a conflict either by giving in or by pretending that there's nothing at all wrong.

8. _____ use intimate knowledge of their partners to get them "where it hurts."

9. _____ attack other parts of their partner's life rather than express their feelings about the object of their dissatisfaction.

10. _____ escape facing up to aggression by shifting the conversation whenever it approaches an area of conflict.

MULTIPLE CHOICE

Identify which element of a clear message is being used in each statement according to the following key:

a. behavioral description
b. interpretation
c. feeling
d. consequence
e. intention

_____ **1.** That's a good idea.

_____ **2.** I'm worried about this course.

_____ **3.** Jim looked angry today.

_____ **4.** I want to talk to you about the $20 you borrowed.

_____ **5.** I notice that you haven't been smiling much lately.

_____ **6.** I don't know whether you're serious or not.

_____ **7.** I'm glad you invited me.

_____ **8.** Ever since then I've found myself avoiding you.

_____ **9.** I'm sorry you didn't like my work.

_____ **10.** I want you to know how important this is to me.

_____ **11.** It looks to me like you meant to embarrass me.

_____ **12.** After the party at Art's, you seemed to withdraw.

_____ **13.** I see you're wearing my ring again.

_____ **14.** From now on you can count on me.

_____ **15.** I've never heard you say a curse word before.

_____ **16.** . . . and since then I've been sleeping at my dad's house.

_____ **17.** Because that occurred, they won't work overtime.

_____ **18.** Dith sighed and looked out the window.

_____ **19.** I'm excited about the possibility.

_____ **20.** I'll get another place to live.

Harcourt Brace & Company

Choose the letter of the personal conflict style that is best illustrated by the behavior found below.

a. avoidance
b. accommodation
c. direct aggression
d. assertion
e. indirect communication
f. passive aggression

_____ **21.** Stan keeps joking around to keep us from talking about commitment.

_____ **22.** "I can't believe you were so stupid as to have erased the disk."

_____ **23.** Even though he wanted to go to the party, Allen stayed home with Sara rather than hear her complain.

_____ **24.** By mentioning how allergic she was to smoke, Joan hoped that her guest would smoke outside.

_____ **25.** "When you smoke inside, I start to cough and my eyes water, so please go out on the balcony when you want to smoke."

_____ **26.** Rather than tell Nick about his frustration over Nick's not meeting the deadline, Howard complained to others about Nick's unreliability while maintaining a smiling front to Nick.

_____ **27.** Carol wouldn't answer the phone after their disagreement because she was afraid it would be Nancy on the other end.

_____ **28.** Faced with his obvious distress, Nikki put her very important work aside to listen to him.

_____ **29.** Even though Nikki could see Kham's distress, she told him she had a deadline to meet in one hour and asked if they could talk then.

_____ **30.** (Sarcastically) "Oh, sure, I *loved* having dinner with your parents instead of going to the party Saturday night."

Harcourt Brace & Company

STUDY GUIDE ANSWERS

CROSSWORD PUZZLE

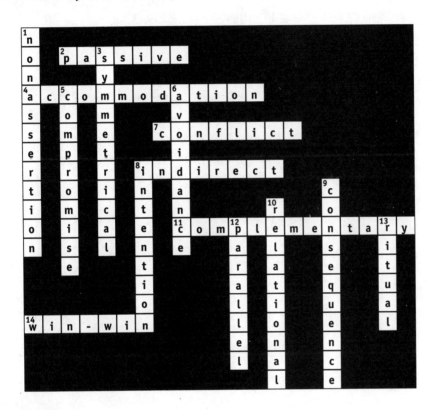

TRUE/FALSE

1.	T	**3.**	F	**5.**	F	**7.**	F	**9.**	F
2.	F	**4.**	T	**6.**	T	**8.**	T	**10.**	F

COMPLETION

1. gunnysackers
2. trivial tyrannizers
3. mind readers
4. trappers
5. avoiders
6. guiltmakers
7. pseudoaccommodators
8. beltliners
9. distractors
10. subject changers

MULTIPLE CHOICE

1. b	**7.** c	**13.** a	**19.** c	**25.** d
2. c	**8.** d	**14.** e	**20.** e	**26.** f
3. b	**9.** c	**15.** a	**21.** a	**27.** a
4. e	**10.** e	**16.** d	**22.** c	**28.** b
5. a	**11.** b	**17.** d	**23.** b	**29.** d
6. b	**12.** b	**18.** a	**24.** e	**30.** f